Bear Valley and Me
Married to a Church Planter

Nancy & Samuel W. Carmack, Ph.D.

Bear Valley
Press

Copyright © 2013 by Bear Valley Press

Colleyville, Texas

All rights reserved.

No part of this book may be reproduced in any form or by any electronic or mechanical means including information storage and retrieval systems, without permission in writing from the author. The only exception is by a reviewer, who may quote short excerpts in a review.

Printed in the United States of America

First Printing: March 2013

Cover Photograph: James Langford Architects

ISBN-978-1-938551-02-4

Contents

Preface 7

Introduction 1

California Dreamin' 3

Reality Bites 15

What About Bob? 35

Movin' On Up 43

Name Game 47

The Band 75

James Brown 107

New Vision 115

Bible for Dummies 135

Getting a Grip 141

Possess the Land 145

School of Rock 159

All Over the World 171

A New Chapter 185

Acknowledgements 189

Preface

How would you write a book describing a wonderful journey God set you on, full of dangerous curves, exhilarating views, and dark, gloomy valleys? That describes this story of starting Bear Valley Community Church.

Initially, Nancy began with the desire to document the history of the first ten years of Bear Valley Community Church. She wanted to immortalize the heroic service of key volunteers and staff members.

She also realized that it gave her a chance to share her story of how church planting not only grows a church, but also develops an individual. There is something spiritually significant about living on the front lines of God's mission. These two elements suggested the format of a travel log. She wanted to describe the scenery on a wonderful journey with God and family.

When she had finished, Nancy asked her husband to help with the rewrite. Sam read these wonderful stories which so profoundly illustrated core principles of the New Paradigm Church (a term he used in a Ph.D. seminar he taught on church development). That is when he got the idea of adding commentary along the way of this journey. His goal was to state succinctly the core principles which Nancy had illustrated.

Nancy and Sam suspect that this book is not finished. If this book meets a need in the market, they plan to write a Second Edition. They hope you, the reader, will add your commentary and help write the next edition. Check out the Facebook page and leave a post.

<u>www.facebook/bearvalleyandme</u>

Introduction

> "In fact, if you know the right thing to do and
> don't do it, that, for you, is evil."
> (James 4:17 Message)

Sometimes you don't want to do something…and then when you do it you find out that it is absolutely the most wonderful thing you've ever done in your entire life.

That's how it was with me and Bear Valley.

I didn't want to start a church. Of course, I didn't know at the time—when I didn't want to do it—that it would be different than I was thinking. If I'd known, well, I surely would have been on board sooner rather than later.

To me church starting meant going door to door meeting people and inviting them to your new church. Just writing that makes me break out in a cold sweat.

Of course if that's what God wanted me to do I'd do it, cold sweat or not. I was wanting to please him.

Truth is, though, I was wanting to please people even more…and inviting them to a new church surely wouldn't please very many people, if they were anything like me, that is.

So here's my story…

Oh, first let me warn you, it can get discombobulated at times. But that's how I am at times: discombobulated.

I hope it and I make sense.

You've just heard from Nancy, who has written the original draft of this book. This is really her story, but in the spirit of "social networking," I'll be adding comments and views along the way in response to this amazing story she has told. My name is Sam. I'll try to stick with this font so you can follow who is doing the writing. I'm the husband and crazy life-partner who got the idea of quitting a perfectly good job to move across three states to a town where we knew no one to start a church from scratch (church planter parlance for "no members").

This is my story of getting out of my box, and doing something where there is no box.

chapter 1

California Dreamin'

> "Yet, O LORD, you are our Father. We are the clay, you are the potter; we are all the work of your hand." (Isaiah 64:8 NIV)

It started in June of 1991.

Southern California sounded appealing. We would go for a few days. I would stay in and near the hotel, relaxing out by the pool some, reading some while Sam would attend a church conference. My parents would take our three and five-year-old and we would get to see California and do my favorite thing three times a day: eat out!

I did not know it would change my life.

While on the flight out there, I decided I might attend at least a session or two. Sam had talked about this Rick Warren fella and he sounded so interesting that I thought maybe I should hear him speak.

I did not know it would change my life.

We had been on "The Track." The Track up. It was a given that Sam would pastor ever bigger churches every few years. After having served as foreign missionaries in Brazil for a short almost three-year term, we came back to the States in the early eighties, and eventually got on The Track. Having finished his doctorate work in New Testament, we moved to precious Chattanooga, Oklahoma (population: 400) where Sam pastored the First Baptist Church. Southwestern Oklahoma, though not known for its beautiful scenery, did become known to us for its wonderful, loving people. Four years later, in 1991, we were in gorgeous central Kentucky, a few miles off the breathtaking Bluegrass Parkway that took us by white-fenced horse farms and rolling hills with lots of trees. I had never lived in a more beautiful place. Sam fit what that county seat church wanted, what with his Ph.D. and his piano-playing wife and their two children. The people there were genteel and southern. The church needed to grow, though, so Sam began devouring any and all literature on church growth that he could get a handle on. That is when he came across the name Rick Warren.

I will never forget the single line in Lyle Schaller's book: It is possible to grow a church through adult conversion, but it requires completely changing the culture of the church. He gave two examples, Saddleback and Willow Creek. As I thought about my church and contemplating changing it, I realized there was one thing which I could not change…the people. My members would always have the same cultural bias toward the people who knew no church culture. I realized I needed to return to my roots of church planting.

As far as I was concerned we were going to southern California to a church growth conference that would help Sam get the church folk motivated to reach the lost and bring backsliders back into the fold. And the conference would be a good break from the kids and housework.

I did not know it would change my life.

Los Angeles is beautiful. The weather is perfect. What's not to like? As far as I was concerned, nothing...except the idea that the earth could move under your feet when you did not expect it. Other than that, it was a great place for a little vacation, nothing more.

I'm glad I changed my mind about just hanging out by the pool at the hotel most of the time.

I'm glad I decided to do some of the conference with Sam.

Well, after I went to that first meeting, I knew I would be doing the whole conference with Sam.

I came very close to attending Saddleback's conference without taking my wife. ...just one more dial of the number, but instead hung up the phone. I'm not sure how this works, whether it is some type of hard wiring of the subconscious mind or an ethereal voice, but what sure looks like a prompting of God from this perspective, gave me the thought, I should invite Nancy, my wife, to go to this conference; after all, it is in sunny California.

I could tell right away that this was going to be an out-of-the-box experience. Here we were, in Mission Viejo, California, driving up to a Lutheran church building for a Baptist church growth conference. Then I find out the reason: the whole conference was being put on by a church that did not even have its own building. What is a church without the steeple? I was soon to find out.

I felt a little too dressy when we were ushered to our seats by a young man dressed in khaki shorts and sandals.

(Remember, this was 1991.) My comfort level improved right away when I saw some old seminary buddies whom we had not seen in years. A conference and a reunion at the same time…and in a heaven-like climate. Not bad.

Then a man got up to welcome everyone and to introduce Rick Warren. It seemed to me that they would have picked a more impressive person to introduce the whole conference. He was a tall, plump man wearing a loud Hawaiian shirt. And he wore no shoes. He was barefoot! This was totally out of my Southern Baptist church-meeting-box. But it did get my attention. As he talked, it began dawning on me that this WAS Rick Warren. This was the man who was getting all the attention for his new and different way of doing church. And he DIDN'T look like a movie star, or even at all like a Billy Graham. Hmm. Interesting. I could tell this would be unlike any church conference I had ever attended.

I went to Saddleback and went away thinking, "I can do this." When I went to Willow Creek I left thinking, "I will never be able to do this." But in the end I found that Willow Creek had the greater impact upon doing church in a way that reached a high percentage of unchurched people. In the first ten years of Bear Valley Community Church, 80% of our growth came from people who had very little or no church background. When I left Bear Valley Community Church, fifteen years later, a survey demonstrated that 50% of the attenders had not attended church for five or more years before coming to Bear Valley. We often measure success for churches by the number of attenders (we had a thousand plus attenders), what I con-

sidered most important was the number of adults finding Christ as central to their life.

After I got over the initial shock that this normal looking, average Joe person was The Rick Warren, he began to impress me. I listened to every word. It was so out of the norm. (More on that later.) I think I must have had a quizzical expression on my face the whole time he was giving that welcome and introduction.

He then turned over the program to his music director, Rick Muchow. Here was a man who was short and bald, not tall, dark and handsome, as you often find leading the music in many big church gatherings. How refreshing. Rick Warren and Rick Muchow were ordinary-looking blokes. No pretense. Everybody was real. It's not that beautiful people cannot be real, but somewhere in my psyche I have found that I respond better when glamour isn't part of the equation.

The music was amazing. I had never heard the songs before, but the tunes were catchy and easy to follow. All of the words were put on screens so that we could all sing along. I particularly remember one that caught my heart on the first go-around. To this day I don't hear, "Lord, I Lift Your Name on High" by Rick Founds without thinking about that first meeting in southern California where my life was changed. The words to the chorus of that song tell the gospel story so clearly and succinctly. Well, I can't resist. Here are the words to that chorus:

> You came from heaven to earth
> To show the way;
> From the earth to the cross,

> My debt to pay;
> From the cross to the grave,
> From the grave to the sky;
> Lord, I lift Your name on high!

After the music part of the service, Rick Warren got up to speak. I was mesmerized. He started talking about how to reach people for Christ. He was making unusual comments, like, "The front porch is dead, folks." How odd. Then he began talking about how witnessing as we know it does not work. It does not work! Whoa! With those words my guilt, both self-imposed and that laid on me by preacher after preacher through the years, began to lift.

Warren was telling us that going door to door witnessing for Jesus, or cornering a fellow co-worker with the Good News of Jesus, was no longer appropriate.

Whoa.

I honestly think that when he began saying those words I heard a collective sigh in the whole crowd.

After talking about the ineffectiveness of door-to-door evangelism, he began talking about the barriers that we put up that keep people from coming to Christ, period. He specifically talked about barriers in a usual Baptist church service. One was the music. Now prior to this I suspected that rock music was evil. Its beat made one think of sensual thoughts (I think that is how the argument went). Well, Rick Warren, whom I was coming to really admire—and credit for being a man of God, though not looking, acting, or speaking like the "old time" men of God—began talking about how people who visit your church like to listen to the kind of music they listened to when they were dating. Never did he put down that kind of music. No. In fact, he promoted it by saying it was the kind of music the church could use to reach people. I was fascinated…and my mind was beginning to open. Imagine, the kind of music I thought was of the devil would be GOOD for the church to use!

This church conference was ringing the Liberty Bell in my soul.

I've written about the experience in California that week in the first part of this book so I will not waste words here except to say that all my guilt and worry over not sharing Christ with total strangers is gone. And oddly, I have had many an opportunity to invite total strangers to our church, and I have gladly done it. When you have a place to invite the "lost" and you know they will feel accepted and loved right at the first, you want to invite them. There is no "ought" or "should" about it. You are compelled to do it—out of LOVE. That is so awesome; as I write this I have goose bumps.

This idea about love propelling one to invite "the lost" to a church like Bear Valley was the answer to a song I had started writing when we lived in Kentucky. The whole story of how I finished that song tells of my struggle, and the answer to that struggle. In Kentucky I wrote this first part:

> I look around and I see the faces of so many people from so many places, they're rushing to and fro. Where do they all go? I look around and I see the tension, it's lined in their brows and that's not to mention the pain that is there,

> the pain they won't share. I look around and wonder what can I do. How can I turn their hearts toward You, hearts that are torn, that are weary and worn? They need You, but what can I do?
>
> I see a world that is lost and dying, I see a world that is hopelessly trying to find some kind of peace of heart and peace of mind. I look around and wonder what can I do. How can I turn their hearts toward You, hearts that are torn, that are weary and worn? They need You, but what can I do? What can I do?

I was stumped as to how to finish that song. I sang it for Sam and told him: That's all there is. He said that some songs don't have a resolution. Well, it got a resolution after we attended that Rick Warren conference and after we had moved to Northeast Tarrant County to start our new church. In fact, within one month of moving here I had it finished. Here's the finish:

> Love them. Just love them. Don't judge them, whatever you do. Love them, first of all love them. Remember that I first loved you.
>
> Think of how you came to know the love of God yourself. Think of how you heard it told by somebody else, someone who cared for you, someone who shared with you, someone who dared to let the love of Christ flow through. Dare to be that someone, too."

To this day, whenever I sing that song, or even think about it for that matter, I'm reminded of how God is in the small stuff, even in little things like words to my little tunes.

Understanding when to love and when to judge presents a real challenge in the Christian's life. Here, let it simply be said that the example of Jesus seemed to lean on the side of love with the irreligious and lean on the side of judgment with the church-going folks. ...if judgment is called for at all.

When I think of loving the "lost" I, of course, think of the "how" of that and I'm reminded that the "how" changes with whomever is considered "the lost." Someone came up with a scale on how close people are to the Gospel, and how that closeness should determine the method of reaching said "lost."

Back in the old days most everyone in America had heard of Jesus and the Bible. When a church held a revival, you were encouraged to bring your friends to "pack the pews." At the closing of each revival service an altar call would be given and many of the community's lost would "come forward." They knew they needed Jesus. Everyone knew what it meant to come to Jesus. On the scale of how close one was to the Gospel, almost everyone in America, well at least in the Texas I knew, were right next to "The Gospel." Nowadays it is drastically different. Really, in the last thirty years the measure of where the general population is on that scale has moved to the far left (-3). Now, on my scale "left" means nothing politically. I'm making my scale like the following ("The Gospel" actually means Knowledge or Awareness of the Gospel):

$$-3\_\_\_-2\_\_\_-1\_\_\_0\_\_\_1\_\_\_2\_\_\_3$$

-3. Skeptic

-2. Curious

-1. Trust the Bible

0. Accept the Gospel

1. Grow

2. Serve

3. Go

This scale changed everything when it came to sharing my faith. The Evangelism Explosion and similar Continuous Witness Training programs which were really popular as recently as the 1980's are rather obsolete now, in my opinion. If you were to place a person, say the lady who runs the local dry cleaners on the scale, she might be to the far left of the words "The Gospel." That would obviously mean she would need a different approach than the let-me-sit-you-down-and-lead-you-to-Jesus approach.

Time would be needed. And inviting her to a safe, barrier-free church service would be totally appropriate.

Obsolete is a rather harsh word. If this upsets you, I hope you will still continue to read. We did learn how to use something like E.E. Here's what I hope you will be asking at this juncture: What do you need to unlearn in order to be more effective in leading adults to Christ? What failures or fears do you harbor which prevents effective communication of the gospel? Who are you trying to please? Whose praise do you care most about?

Nancy had to overcome the repeated failures experienced in door-to-door evangelism. She also had to overcome the opinion of authority figures in her past concerning music style in worship.

I remember in Brazil watching a group of Christians at the beach. Beach attire in Brazil was as near to nudity as possible. The method of handling beach attire for this group was to wear street clothes while swimming. It looked kind of silly to me. Then the thought crossed my mind: I wonder what I do that looks silly to my non-Christian friends? What do we need to unlearn?

The scale, which Nancy referred to, was created by James F. Engel. Google it. It was designed primarily for overseas missionaries ministering to new fields. Probably the biggest change in thinking needed in North America is that most of our culture is more like a mission field. Here's an interesting fact we learned in Texas (the Bible Belt): The largest unchurched people-group in Texas is White/Anglo.

I was seeing that this new kind of Saddleback church was a great way for a person like me to bring my acquaintances to Christ, or at least to a closer position on the "Knowledge of the Gospel Scale." Anybody can invite anybody to a church service. And that "anybody" meant me! 'Course if the service was packed with ritual that only the initiated knew, the visiting "anybody" would feel awkward, and this "anybody" would feel awkward "feeling" for them.

So this background of guilt over not sharing my faith with programs such as EE and CWT was gloriously being lifted at this California Rick Warren conference.

chapter 2

Reality Bites

> "Trust in the LORD with all your heart and lean not on your own understanding; in all your ways acknowledge him, and he will make your paths straight." (Proverbs 3:5–6 NIV)

The whole conference was eye opening to me. I can remember walking back to our rental car to go to the hotel thinking about it all. It is so true, I thought. People are not turned off by God. They are turned off by the church. It is a foreign culture to them. We can reach people for Christ. We just need to take the barriers down that they encounter when they come to our church services. Of course, we can't take ALL the barriers down, as Jesus, himself, is still "the stumbling block" as the Bible tells us in 1 Cor. 1:23. But we need to make the Gospel accessible, not inaccessible. And the beauty of it was, we could do so without compromising any of the Gospel message. Many of our traditions were just that: traditions. It was as if I was seeing Christianity being dunked into the 1990's and on into the 21st century. And we could do it, Sam and I. When we were at supper that night and he started talking about one day starting our own church, and implementing those things we were hearing from Rick Warren, I was so on board. It was as if I were on a high. I could do church, and actually love it at the same time. Kind of like having my cake and eating it, too, I thought. Wisely, we knew we could not just return to our Kentucky home and change everything, but we could start opening the minds of some folks and maybe tweak a few things so as to reach some newcomers for Christ. Then later, we'd go somewhere and do "this new church-thing." How exciting.

And as is often the case, we tend to think other people are like us and are having the same reactions. Wrong. On the way to a wives' luncheon that second day of the conference I found out not everyone was smitten with Rick Warren and his new-fangled church.

"I don't want to start a church! I don't want to start a church! Everything was going well. I liked my life! Help me, girls. Am I the only one who is rebelling?" She kept talking, venting. I sat next to her in the back seat of the car. We were all strangers. If I heard her name I have forgotten it. Odd that she kept talking and almost crying to strangers. I wanted to silence her. Well, not really. She was daring to say what she felt. Like me, she must have thought others were feeling her feelings.

It had been a long and interesting morning. The husbands and wives had been together listening in what I thought was all rapt attention to Rick Warren and his tales of starting Saddleback Community Church in sunny southern California. I had been extremely impressed with him and what he had to say about church. Now my high was being deflated. I did not know what to say to that young preacher's wife. I guess I must have said something in sympathy to her. As I recall the other wives said things like, "God won't lead you where he won't be with you." Or "Hang in there, maybe your husband is just needing to talk about it to you, and maybe he won't do something rash immediately." (It wasn't until a month later that I fully empathized with that gal.)

Though that conference in Mission Viejo, California was what got me to want to start Bear Valley Church, I clearly needed time to assimilate it all. Prior to that conference any talk of starting a church scared me. I had known that Sam had helped start a church near Houston, as part of a seminary practicum before we knew each other. In Brazil, he had helped start a few churches and was frustrated when his job description called for him to do just behind-the-desk work. I knew in the back of my mind that church starting was where his heart was, but I guess I was in denial, because any time he would bring the subject up I would inwardly cringe. It sounded too scary. Odd, that I did not have that feeling when we went to my version of Timbuktu (Brazil). It was an adventure—and of course, I had felt "called." But any talk of starting a church here in the States did not give me a sense of calling, just a sense of fear. I knew it would mean knocking on strangers' doors to invite them to come to a new church that they might think is an upstart of whatever, maybe some cult. It would mean that people might think Sam was doing it because he could not hack it on "The Track." It would mean people might think who knows what, and I was all about wondering what people might think. That is a whole other book someday, but, of course, will be treated a lot in this one, since I am its author.

Well, Rick Warren was getting me on the bandwagon. Maybe it was because of the idea that "The front porch is dead" so I would not have to go to strangers' doors to "drum up business." But it was more than that. I was beginning to get the vision. Beginning to see that you COULD reach people by bringing them to a safe place, that did not have hoops for them to jump through so they could come to Christ. I was beginning to see just what those hoops were and how church culture is so foreign to the unchurched out there and it doesn't have to be! Mmm. It was so exciting, and I was feeling the excitement almost at a fever pitch.

Ah, but my mountain top experience was to come to an end as I faced the real world. We came back to beautiful Kentucky with its genteel people. Those gentry, however, had not been to that life-changing conference and probably wouldn't want us messing things up with our newly learned new-fangled California ways. We were smart, though. We knew that Springfield Baptist should not be transitioned into a seeker-sensitive congregation. That would not be fair to the people there.

If we were to have a nontraditional approach to church we would need to start our own.

Here let me say that we were not mad at that church for not being able to change. It should not have been changed. (This is subject matter for another book—how traditional churches are traditional because that is the way most of the people there like them. It would be unfair for a pastor to come back from a conference and proceed to set everything on its tail. (Sadly, some pastors do that.)

The principle here: You can't change culture; you can only kill it and start a new one.

Here is advice for Church Planters... Be very careful about selecting your initial group of members—your Core Group or Launch Team. The type of people they are will probably determine the culture of your church. A classic mistake is to take a group of people from an already existing church and then be surprised that they want the new church to be like their old church. At least get people from many different churches so they bring competing cultures; better yet, find several new Christians or non-Christians to be part of your launch team. They will help greatly in creating an environment less hostile to your nonchurch guests. Back to Nancy...

I had been thinking that though we would definitely start a new "seeker church," we would not do it for a while, maybe two or three years. That way, I could be the first lady of the county seat church a little longer and then we would move on having served a respectable four or five years. I am all about respectability.

The month after we came back to Kentucky from the California conference, the kids and I went to stay with my parents in East Texas for a week. We were having a good visit when Sam called and told me that he wanted to resign the church the very next Sunday. What?! What?! Needless to say, that sent me into a tizzy. We had only been in Springfield seventeen months and that was too soon to leave, in my opinion. It was not respectable. What will people think? And what will my parents think? And it would be crazy. "Crazy" is the word I kept coming back to. Not only did Sam want to resign immediately, he wanted us to move in with his parents in Oklahoma for however long it took to decide where we might go and start this seeker church. He had planned it out; that we could put the kids in the Hinton, Oklahoma schools in August so they wouldn't start late. I could see his reasoning. It made sense in my head, but certainly not my heart. All of the late-night calls he made when I was at White Haven (my parents' country home in East Texas) were upsetting my parents because they were upsetting me. Really, that's when I started my worst "basket-case" period. Ah, it would sound as if Sam were making me a basket case. How dare he? He was not, though. Every time we talked on the phone about his resignation, he would gently point out why the time was right to do it then. He would tell me honestly that I could say, "No, we cannot do it now," and he would honor my wishes of staying put a while longer. I could not say that though, because I knew it was just my own insecurities that were driving me to not do what I really knew we should do.

I still have some of the notes I wrote in the wee hours of the mornings during that White Haven time at my parents' country home in July of 1991. I have decided that I will include some of those notes here. It seemed only appropriate that I wrote them on some Zorial tablets I found at my folks' home. Zorial is the pesticide my father used to sell before he retired. For promotional purposes he got boxes and boxes of those tablets. He would give them away to all of his customers and we would get to keep the rest. They were everywhere, all over the house. My mother, my sister and I did not have to buy notepads for years. We used them for everything: grocery lists, to-do lists, you name it. And in the summer of 1991, I used them to cry out to God, and for God to reach down to me.

This is risky, I know, to share this "Zorial journal," because I am letting you, the reader, into my mind and thoughts and into what I believed God was telling me. Here goes:

On July 26, 1991 at around 11:00 p.m. I wrote the following:

To move now… can it be right?

Help Sam to know. Help me to know.

And help me cope, Lord.

Help me to have strength and wisdom—as to what to say, what to do, how to feel.

Lord, help Sam know what to say and what to do with Springfield BC. With Vic and Ruth, John and Jenny, Vedie and Jeff, Charlotte and Howard, Leon and Karen, Elaine, Mary and Barney, and especially Dr. Howard and "Aunt Dorane."

Show us the way to go. When. How. Where.

Should we go now?

Later in the night I wrote:

Lord, are we crazy? Is this OUR desire? Or is it really Yours? Are You leading us to move now? Now? And if so, why?

Why now?

I'm open for some answers.

Help me.

I "hear" (my eyes fell on this)—2 Corinthians 2:10 (Good News Bible—that is on hand in my parents' guest room), "I am content with weaknesses, insults, hardships, persecutions and difficulties for Christ's sake. For when I am weak, then I am strong."

And 1 Timothy 1:12, "I give you strength for your work."

Lord, be with Sam. Lead him. Clearly. Clearly.

1 Peter 3:14, "even if you should suffer for doing what is right, how happy you are! Do not be afraid of men and do not worry—But have reverence for Christ in your hearts, and make him your Lord. Answer people of the hope in you with gentleness and respect."

We've only been in Springfield seventeen months!

1 Peter 4:12, 13 "Don't be surprised at the painful test you are suffering… Be glad you are sharing Christ's suffering."

Verse 19; "Trust yourself completely to the Creator."

I hate to leave our church after being there only 17 months.

It doesn't seem right. In fact, I think we ought to stay longer.

But Sam doesn't, and he is the one who decides ultimately.

I will trust him.

At 1:30 a.m. I wrote…

Why I want to:

<u>Stay</u>

-church would be shocked

-looks better on resume
-don't want to let pulpit committee and friends down
-church is doing well
-beautiful country
-relatively safe
- won't be understood if we go
- friends (Harrisons, Howards, Reynolds, Bradys, Tingles, etc.)
- Mother and Daddy won't respect Sam if we leave

Why I want to…
<u>Go</u>
-Sam is unhappy
-church is difficult
-time spent on maintenance rather than reaching out
-way too many expectations on Sam
- Sam wants to start church for baby boomers
- Sam has always dreamed of starting a church

Things we've done:
-Master Life
-2 mission trips
-led people to witness
-gotten Mary to counseling
-directory
-giving increased
-attendance increased
-talked to Bobby and others about dating

Leaving now is good. It will
- stir the church up.
- be good because power group is not in power now
-mean we'll get on with our lives

Leaving now is hard because…
-it's hard.
-shattering of a dream, we'll not go to a big prestigious church someday

Fears for future. Here they are, Lord.
-schooling for Will and Laura
-adjustments for Will and Laura
-failure: that it won't work

Excitements:
-Will and Laura will have really good schooling (?)
-Sam and I will work as a team
-I'll stretch in area of music
-Freedom from tradition
-I will share Christ more?
-Faith will grow
-Maybe we'll move closer to family?

Later that week I wrote the following. I felt as if it was God was telling me:

Nancy, you agonize over others' reactions to what you're doing. "What will they think? How can I get them to understand or approve?"

Look to Me. Be more concerned about MY approval than anyone's. <u>Seek my face.</u> <u>Trust Me.</u> <u>Completely</u>.

Don't look around. Get focused. Draw near to Me and I will draw near to you. Trust Me and I will show you great and mighty things that you know not of. Abandon yourself to Me. Don't worry. And don't lean on your own understanding. I will direct your path.

Others will not understand, or approve, or accept this as right and proper. What do you have to do with them? Look to Me. Seek Me first. The fear of man is a snare. Commit your way unto Me. As you received Me, so walk in Me. By faith. Don't fret about what others will say. Look to Me. Cast your cares upon Me.

You did not choose Me. I chose you.

You are chosen to proclaim my wonderful acts (1 Peter 2:9).

Don't try to figure it out.

You're getting sick because you're looking with human eyes.

Seventeen months IS short—but trust Me. I allowed you to be in Springfield for seventeen months. What is the time to you? You are to trust ME.

I will lead you and I will guide you in the way that you should go.

My ways are not your ways. Don't try to understand.

LEAN HARD.

I will take care of those you love.
— God

So that is what I wrote. Typing it just now has been awesome. I'm so very glad I kept it all. Wow. I wrote it, and now I see how it all has been happening. I'm teary as I type. A wonderful teary. All I can say is "Thank You, Lord."

Throughout these notes, the Lord seemed to be leading me, tenderly, to do the out-of-the-box-thing. When I shared with my parents all of this, and that I thought Sam was right, I could tell their love and concern for me was foremost and that surely Sam must be having a mid-life crisis. They knew of the long phone calls, and the sleepless nights. I was (am) their daughter. They wanted what was best for me and their grandchildren. They did not try and talk me into talking Sam out of it, though, so I credit them with trusting him, and me.

Sam resigned. He did it while I was in Texas, which really was good. It spared me, in a way, the initial reactions of church members who would clearly not understand. I was going to reap the on-second-thought reactions, and they were not, "Oh, we understand. You must do what God calls you to do." Well, there were certain people who voiced those thoughts. For the most part, though, the kind Kentucky folk were bewildered as to how God would lead us to them and then suddenly move us on. Ooo, yes, Sam and I were doing something very unpopular. My people pleasing ways were being challenged... I couldn't explain our decision well enough to satisfy anyone. I began having insomnia. Never before had I empathized with folks who just could not fall asleep. Now I can empathize big time.

Lack of sleep did not help in my mood. No longer was I excited about this new venture. I was scared, and even mad. Mad at Sam and mad at myself that I would let us do this crazy thing. I mean, we had a cushy job at the biggest church in the county, and we lived in this great old two-story parsonage that was <u>not</u> right next to the church. I was loved and revered as the talented preacher's wife. Clearly I enjoyed the prestige. Now we had gone out to California—where all traditional values are questioned—and we had succumbed to the new-fangled Rick Warren way of thinking. And I was stuck. I had said out there on the west coast that I had wanted to start a new church. It must have been that guacamole burger that got into my head out there, plus all the casual folks we met. Good grief. What had I gotten myself into?

Deep down, though, I really knew I had been wooed by God to do this new thing. Deep down I knew it was so right. But right does not mean easy.

We said our good-byes and left beautiful Kentucky.

I really need to thank Nancy for accepting the most difficult task of a life-partner... Don't Be A Dream Killer! Both of us have learned to help the other achieve life-long goals. I know she has done this much more than I have. Honestly, I didn't fully appreciate how hard it was for her. I didn't realize I was about to ask her to do one of the hardest thing a woman can do... move in with her in-laws.

Here's a principle: A prerequisite for ministry is a good marriage. This is especially true for church planting.

Expect extreme pressure on your marriage. We even had one "good friend" who thought maybe it might be time for Nancy to divorce me.

Since we did not know where we were going to start the church the logical place to move was back home with the folks. Now we were no spring chickens. It's only lately that I've really wondered what my in-laws must have thought when Sam called them up and asked (told?) them we were moving in. They were very gracious. Sam's brother and two boys had lived with them for two years in the eighties while he fought for custody. I guess they couldn't turn us away.

The children and I moved in with Nana and Daddy-Bob before Sam did. School was starting and we had to get them enrolled. That left Sam with the arduous job of packing up all our belongings and moving them from Springfield, Kentucky to Hinton, Oklahoma. My job of getting settled in Nana's house seemed minuscule in comparison.

Nana and Daddy-Bob's house was big, yes... but at thirty-nine years old, and with two young children, I really had some trouble moving in with my in-laws, no matter how big the house was and how wonderful the in-laws were. More insomnia. More bad mood. Still the basket-case.

I did not know how long we would live there... maybe if I had known it would turn out to be just two months I would have gotten a good night's sleep. Who knows. It was a challenge for me, though. Sam was busy researching places that might need a "seeker sensitive church"—as Rick Warren called them—and I was busy trying to stay busy, and not under foot—with my two little ones.

I would like to mention, there are some phrases which I would never use if starting another church. One is Seeker Church or Seeker Sensitive Church. Another is, a Church for the Unchurched. Another... Seeker Service. I now believe the Sunday morning primetime worship period, 11:00 a.m., should be a worship service which honors 1 Corinthians 14:23. Does the worship service appeal to any group of people outside the church culture? If it doesn't, it's time to redesign the worship format. We learned that you can worship in a way that invites the nonbelieving guest into God's presence. The best expression of this principle comes from Bill Hybels (although be careful about adopting his format). I paraphrase, we try to remove every barrier we can, so they can consider the barrier which matters, the stumbling-block, Jesus Christ. For this book we will use the term Seeker for those who are curious about Christ but feel like an outsider to church culture.

I also need to say something about the word "conversion." I grew up in a context where conversion was seen as an event. At Bear Valley we have learned that it is more of a process. We did help people to have events, or key moments, in their process of conversion, such as baptism, prayer (telling God that you trust him and want to change) and confession (telling others about a new found and growing faith). Let's get back to the story...

We looked at Kansas City, Kansas and considered—but never "looked at"—places like Phoenix, Denver, and some I have forgotten. In the course of study Sam spoke with a friend with the Southern Baptist North American Mission Board. He suggested we look at southwest Houston and northeast Tarrant County—near Fort Worth. I was elated. Houston and Fort Worth were in Texas, my home state!!! Never had we considered Texas. It was Bible Belt. There are too many churches there already, right? Joe from the NAMB said, no. Oh yes there are lots of churches… practically one on every corner. They are NOT reaching the unchurched, though. They just trade members back and forth, growing by what is called "transfer growth" or "feeder growth." This was music to my ears.

This term Feeder Church usually refers to smaller churches, which feed the larger churches. Once the children in the smaller churches become teenagers, the family transfers to the larger church where the cool youth program resides. The larger church looks successful because of transfer growth from churches upon which it is feeding. I believe that most mega-churches grow from transfer growth. That certainly was the case in the 1990's. Bear Valley started across the freeway from the largest church in the county. In our first year we baptized 35 adults, the same number of adults baptized in that large church across the freeway. We averaged less than 100 in attendance. They averaged well over 2,000 in attendance. Both churches are needed.

Nancy was saying…

We traveled to Houston. It would have been a great, wonderful place for me to consider, except for one big thing: my identical twin, Peggy, had lived there all her married life, and had died there in 1989. When I went back to go through her things after the funeral, people would look at me as if I were a ghost. I did not want to be the ghost walking around town, and I did not want the pain of going where Peggy and I always would hang out. Being there, to check it out for a possible church start was almost too much for me. We would have been in a different part of town, but I still felt a heaviness about the whole thing. Of course, the working through of that grief might have been hastened had we moved to Houston, but I am glad that maybe God thought I needed not to hasten it, since He did not lead us there. The whys and wherefores of all of that are only known to God, and I'm glad. I've learned through the years to follow His lead, not to analyze it to death.

Then we looked at the Dallas Metroplex. Now we're talking. I had always considered Dallas the hub of the universe. As a child my family would travel there at least three or four times a year to see one set of grandparents who lived in Oak Cliff in southwest Dallas and the other set of grandparents who lived thirty miles away in Kaufman. As we would drive north from the Rio Grande Valley and finally see the Dallas skyline, my sister and I would start to squeal. We loved it.

The mere idea of possibly moving to the Metroplex abated my insomnia.

During that time of decision making—determining where to go, and how to do, etc.— Sam got a chance to visit Willow Creek Community Church near Chicago. There he saw how Bill Hybels was reaching the unchurched by the thousands. With both Rick Warren and Bill Hybels' churches as models, Sam was really getting a vision of what he wanted his own church to be. As we will see in the telling of this story, it borrowed from both Warren and Hybels, yet became uniquely Carmack. Well, of course, uniquely God's. Thankfully God was letting Sam (and me) in on the creation. As Sam says, "That's the way God does it. He lets you in on the creating part."

I've never seen this principle expressed in Church Planting literature, but I think it may be one of the most important. When designing your strategy for church development, be sure to take into consideration the key leader, the church planter. The passion and skills of this person should parallel the style of the church being planted.

Now the question may arise somewhere in the course of this story; How could we support ourselves? The average church starter might be consumed with how to pay for everything a new church would need, besides his/her own household needs. Our answer to that question is wonderful. Sam had bought some stock while we were living in Chattanooga, Oklahoma, before our Springfield stay, and that stock soared in value. Our God is a big God. So big that when we started the church we knew we could go without a salary for a good five years. It would be a tight budget of $38,000 a year (1990 dollars), but my goodness, is my life a dream-life or what?

It would have been hard to do this if I hadn't learned how to manage a home budget. We used Larry Burkett's envelope system. I have kept those hand written records to remind me of the importance of developing basic life skills in order to achieve spiritual goals.

In spite of having our basic needs met financially we did not have our wants met necessarily. We put ourselves on a budget when we left our Kentucky home and moved in with "the folks," so that we could see where our money was going, and so as not to get overdrawn. We recorded every single expense down to the piece of gum from the gum machine. I found out really quickly that recording every cent spent meant NOT buying that gum for the sole reason being I did not want to record it. Where I really cut down, though, was on my consumption of Dr. Peppers. Recording every single can drunk showed me that I drank way more of those than I should. Mmm. Withdrawal was not easy.

I need to give special mention to the Baptist General Convention of Texas and Tarrant Baptist Association. They graciously gave money for the first three years of the church of about $70,000. Others, not members of the church, gave about $80,000 during the first few years. These amounts are fairly typical; expect to need to raise about $100,000 to $200,000 during the first five years of the church. In order to plant a church, you have to be willing to ask others to support it.

chapter 3

What About Bob?

> "Before a word is on my tongue you know it completely, O LORD. You hem me in — behind and before; you have laid your hand upon me. Such knowledge is too wonderful for me, too lofty for me to attain." (Psalms 139:4-6 NIV)

The idea that we might move to North Texas put a whole new skip in my step. The more we looked at that area, the more interested Sam became. As for me, my interest was practically innate.

I had not realized Nancy's difficulty with Houston until reading this book. That's a little embarrassing, but reminds me of the importance of prayer. After I had gathered information, it looked like either S.W. Houston, Kansas City or N.E. Tarrant County of DFW area, in that order. I took one day to pray and fast. I really don't understand fasting, but just to be safe, I do it on really important decisions or needs. At the end of that day there was a strong sense that we should change our list of priorities and put N.E. Tarrant County at the top of the list, instead of Houston. I always look for both a subjective and objective leading of God's will. This was the subjective part. Nancy's story will lay the objective pathway.

Sam made a trip to the Dallas-Fort Worth area in August, 1991 and did a "windshield survey." That is when a person drives around and visually assesses the demographics of an area. I call it cruising around to see what the area looks like. Though there were a lot of churches in the area, to Sam they all looked very traditional from the outside. It was exciting for him to see lots of subdivisions being developed, which meant a lot of people were moving into the area.

I especially wanted to find an area in the south which had lots of people moving in from the north and west. Why? ...looking for people with less church background. I also had read that the church planter tends to attract people within five years of his age. I looked for a place with lots of younger Baby Boomers... Classic Rock.

Sam decided to call the Dallas Baptist Association and see how interested it was in helping us start a church. He was told that Dallas County had all the new churches it wanted. No more were needed.

Dum de dum dum. That would have been the tune I would play if I had heard that response. Not Sam.

Now, in the Bible belt where there does seem to be a church on every corner, that response would seem natural. Sam had studied statistics of the area prior to that phone call and he knew that yes, churches were abundant. What he also knew, and evidently the Dallas Association did not, was that there were thousands upon thousands of people who were not being reached for Christ. New churches WERE needed... but not the kind of churches of which the unchurched would steer clear. Sam had known of many studies in that regard. One such study had asked several people who did not consider themselves Christians to look at a stack of pictures and take out the one that they thought looked most like a typical churchgoer. The winning picture was not the one of the father playing ball. Or the young person helping an older person across the street. Or the young man painting an old building. Or the older woman with her grandchildren at a playground. Or even the middle-aged man sitting reading the Bible. The winning picture was of an older lady in dressy clothes sitting in an elegant living room with a cat on her lap. She was looking directly at the camera and not smiling. Most Christians that I know would be surprised that that is the picture that "won" the "Christian prize." Surveys and studies show, though, that that is just how the non-Christian of today sees the Christian. Smug. Elegant. Judgmental. Certainly not what we would want him/her to see.

I should mention the classic error of most pastors. They think building a conversion-growth church means putting a rock band on stage. I hope you see in this book that a church, which grows by adult conversion, has to be willing to adopt some of the culture of the irreligious. I remembered when we lived in Brazil, many of the churches we visited had organs powered by foot pumps; yes, a pump organ. No one, except my wife, knew how to play one, but some stateside Christian who had visited these churches thought they needed an organ, thus the donation. Sometimes it is best not to accept gifts. How much better it would have been for the churches to use the instrument of the people: guitars. The question of how far you push this principle of cultural adoption is very important and very dangerous, because there are some elements of culture which are malevolent.

Sam knew Dallas County needed some new churches even if the Dallas Baptist Association did not, well, back in the early '90's. Now, as I write this (in 2012) the Dallas Baptist Association has many new "seeker-sensitive" churches, and is VERY actively trying to reach the unchurched for Christ.

That phone call to the DBA, however disappointing, was the first time Sam heard the name "Bob Roberts." Sam was told that he needed to meet Bob, who lived in Tarrant County and that Bob might could help us in our church-starting desire. Sam filed that away in his brain, little knowing how important it would be.

He then contacted Larry Rose, the Director of Missions (which could be translated "executive officer") of the Tarrant Baptist Association. Now here was a man after Sam's own heart. Larry Rose had a passion for reaching people for Christ. Still, however, Sam felt Rose was at first giving him a polite, but "no thanks" interview, until he discovered Sam's background. (Sam later found out that The Association receives about a thousand applications a year to start churches!) When Rose found out that Sam had already secured his own finances and that Sam had a Ph.D., well, Rose said, "We have a vision of hundreds of new churches here in Tarrant County," he told Sam, and "You need to talk to Bob Roberts." That name again.

A few days later Sam was talking on the phone to a person in the offices of the Baptist General Convention of Texas and he also said, "You need to talk to Bob Roberts."

By that time Sam was convinced that he needed to hunt this Bob Roberts down.

"Can you tell me how I can find Bob Roberts?" Sam asked.

"As a matter of fact, he's sitting right here in my office," he replied.

So that was the beginning of our history with Bob.

Bob and Sam set an appointment to meet. From that meeting, Bob's church, Northwood Church in Keller, was poised to sponsor us. Bob was surely impressed with Sam (of course!) but still there must have been reservations on Bob's part. Prior to sponsoring our church, Northwood had tried two times to plant a church and both times the church starter had resigned. The very fact that Bob would take a chance on Sam after those disappointments speaks highly of both men.

Actually, I think maybe Bob decided I was the least worse choice. I later found out he had real questions about my people-skills. I am a bit of an Introvert and Bob an extreme Extrovert, the kind of personality I tend to shy away from. However, I should mention that most church planters are not Introverts (on the Myer Briggs scale I'm INTP). This meant that I needed to adopt a strategy that accepted the Introvert part of my personality. Here are a few thoughts if this applies to you: I would spend most all of Saturday by myself so I was ready to spend Sunday with people. As we grew, I focused on a few key relationships and developed them deeply. Many of these became staff members of the church. As the church grew I carefully hired people different from myself but similar enough that I enjoyed being with them; in other words, I hired Extro-

verts. The church grew to an average attendance of 650 before I left. I had found two key associate pastors who could carry hundreds of relationships. I could only keep up about 70 relationships effectively. The strength that I brought was in the area of deep thinking and insightful decisions. Someone wrote a book on leadership styles. My style was The Wise Leader. Okay, why am I telling you all this? Learn to understand yourself. This will give you a major clue as to how to design your organization. Some common things to look at: Myers Briggs, Devotional Pathways, DISC, Leadership Styles, Love Languages, to name a few.

Speaking highly of Bob Roberts is not hard. Here is a man that is larger than life. When he walks in the room, everyone else pales in comparison. His outgoing nature and big exuberant smile, however, do not reveal the very sensitive man underneath that seeming bravado. In fact, it is not bravado, it is genuine love and enthusiasm at seeing whomever is in the room. And he is very smart. He saw in Sam Carmack a capable church planter and did not hesitate to encourage his church members to support Sam however they could.

I don't want to get ahead of myself here, so I will not tell of that generous help from Northwood until later. I do want to give a hearty "thank you," to magnanimous Bob for all his support at the get-go. It will never be forgotten. Without it, Bear Valley would have just remained a dream and never have become a reality. I should note here that since the early nineties, he and his wife, Nikki, have been involved in helping church-starts all over the world.

What About Bob

Bob recently wrote:

I love Bear Valley and Sam Carmack. It was the first church we "helped" start. Church planters start churches, and Sam started it. We helped along with other churches and people. It was Bear Valley that got my feet in the water of church multiplication. It showed me it could be done and I could be a part of it. I always pass by Bear Valley and smile every time I see it and thank God I was there when it was born.

— Bob Roberts, Northwood

chapter 4

Movin' On Up

> "Delight yourself in the LORD and he will give you the desires of your heart." (Psalms 37:4 NIV)

So God was opening the door for us to move to the Metroplex. I was ecstatic. It would mean many things: moving to a place of our own, living near my parents, and, of course, getting back to the Lone Star State. What could be better? Not much in my estimation.

It was good that I was excited about the move because there were some hard things facing us that I had not really considered. No ready friends, for example. Everywhere else we had moved we found a welcoming committee eager to help us with the details of getting settled as well as with the emotions of being uprooted. Though we had a sponsor church, Northwood, we moved miles away from it so we did not have the close proximity of new friends and new help.

We were also moving from a tiny town to a huge metropolitan city. I had thought I would enjoy the anonymity that would bring, but I found myself missing being recognized as "the preacher's wife." Hmm. I had so complained about the fishbowl existence of the clergy life that

I had not appreciated the benefit of it. I did, though, relish not living in a parsonage. However small and impersonal the apartment, it did afford a certain feeling of "my own place" where no one you know has lived before. There were not the comments of how I decorated (and cleaned) the place compared to my predecessor. Whew.

I must admit, the biggest surprise in the start-up phase of Bear Valley was the utter sense of loneliness and lack of identity. I don't know any good solution to avoid this if you are going to do something rather unique. Here's what we did: We set about meeting people and making friends of people who don't like church. We hung out with our neighbors who didn't like church. I tried to lose the First Baptist Church look and speech. I even learned to laugh at dirty jokes; although, I have refrained from telling them.

I did find myself with some culture shock. Really. Small town life is very different than big city life. And our definition of "small town" is not everyone's definition. Oprah Winfrey called Amarillo, Texas a small town. She has a different definition than mine. After returning from the mission field (Brazil in 1983) we lived until '85 in Hinton, Oklahoma, population: 1100; from '86 to '90 in rural Chattanooga, Oklahoma, population 400; then to our new Kentucky home, Springfield, population 3,000. Moving to the Metroplex took some getting used to. Besides the anonymity, there is the potential crime and there are the potential fender benders. We were reminded of that every time we watched TV. I remember how the tall, dark and handsome lawyer from the Kondos and Kondos Law Firm would tell us how we could get a settlement if we were involved in a car wreck. Jim Adler, the "tough, smart lawyer," also could help us if we'd been a victim of a crime, or ephedrine, the weight loss drug that caused heart problems. Brian Loncar was there for us, too. And KAY Clinic could fix our bodies up. These commercials were not reassuring. They were scaring me.

I finally did get accustomed to driving in lots of freeway traffic. The idea that my kids would someday learn to drive in this traffic, though, did not comfort me. Writing this in retrospect has made me see that it was not as bad as I had anticipated. Nothing usually is.

Before I could be an effective church planter. I had to first learn to become a mature husband. I don't know where you stand on the issue of authority in the home. Who has the final decision on issues of career, location, etc. No matter where it may be, here's a truth which I hope you'll take to heart: Major decisions must be shared by both the husband and wife. Early in our marriage I learned that I needed to encourage Nancy to speak the full truth about what she could endure. I need to include that information in choosing what I would do. Husbands, please find a way for your wife to speak her full mind on these issues in a safe, loving environment. Husbands, learn to affirm your wife's fears and emotions. She needs to know that her husband believes that they are real and justified. This will put both of you in a much better position to make the hard changes needed in your life to be fully effective for God.

Church puts a great deal of stress on a marriage. This stress will either enhance the relationship in your marriage or break it.

chapter 5

Name Game

> "By the grace God has given me, I laid a foundation as an expert builder…"
> (1 Corinthians 3:10 NIV)

So how do you start a church from scratch when you do not have to go door to door? One word: Mail. You send your prospects enticing invitations to come check out this enticing new church.

Oh, but I'm getting ahead of myself. Before the mailers, and before the church services, we had to get together a core of people to help us. Oh, and before that we had to come up with a name. Yes. We decided that as the preacher and preacher's wife we would come up with a name before we would let anybody else give his/her ideas on what it should be. It is so much easier deciding something when only two people are doing it. Two heads are better than seventeen…in many decisions.

We also described our church in writing. This is pretty common today. Strategy, Vision, Purpose, Beliefs… When I coach church planters, I explain that they need to articulate clearly, without effort, not only a thirty minute sale of their vision, but a three minute sale and a thirty second sale. You use the latter with everyone you meet and look for a gleam of interest in his or her eyes. Some call this the Elevator Sale. It's all about relationships. Looking for people who want to be your friend and then finding key people who can become leaders in the church. People don't join a church plant. They join the church planter. But I'm getting a bit ahead, how did we get the name, Bear Valley Community Church?

Naming anything is very important. Daunting, actually. A name can be a definition and a description. A name itself has the power to attract or repel, especially repel. Of course, a rose by any other name would smell as sweet, but I'm glad it wasn't given the name "slug."

What should our church name be? We found that searching for a name, though hard, was actually quite fun. We looked at names of streets and particularly names of subdivisions. Evidently much thought has gone into names like "Woodland Hills' and "Brook Meadows," yet there seem to be no woods, hills, brooks, or meadows in those neighborhoods. I guess it did not matter what one called oneself. It just had to sound appealing.

I wanted to avoid names which identified with organized religion, Bible churches or charismatic churches.

Okay, we wanted a good sounding name. Location might be something to consider also. It would be in the northeastern part of Tarrant County. The words "north" and "east" might play a part in our new name. With that in mind we somehow narrowed it down to North Haven Church. We both liked the word "haven." My parents had named their house and land out in the country of east Texas "White Haven." Haven was really what we wanted our church to be. What a great name, "North Haven." It had location in it and a meaningful descriptive word. It would be a Safe Haven to the unchurched interested in Jesus. We had already decided it would not have Baptist in the name, since, unfortunately a lot of people—especially those we were going to try to reach—had a bad connotation of the word "Baptist." We had considered calling it a "community" church, but when we discovered that Metropolitan Community Church was a gay church, we ruled that out. (At that time that church was the only church we knew of that used the word "community." This later changed and "community" became a common term for many types of churches.) So North Haven Church was our decision. We even sent out a mailer, market-testing that name. We also called ourselves that to Northwood Church members who might help us get started.

Alas, "North Haven" was not to be. From that mailer, we discovered that name was identified with the gay church movement. Now we wanted to open ourselves up to everyone, but we did not want to be known as a gay church. However judgmental that may sound we began looking for another name. In our search, we began noticing how many schools and businesses had "Bear Creek" in their names. We found no church, however, listed in the yellow pages with that name. Hmm. Maybe we were the ones God was waiting for—to take it.

"Bear Creek Church" sounded pretty good. Then Sam decided to put the name "valley" into it. Water runoff (technical "valley") into Bear Creek fairly well defined our initial area. Oo, and I liked the word "valley." It had a good feel about it. And valleys seemed safe and secure. Of course "valley" could also mean a low time in one's life.

How appropriate. We could reach people in the valleys of their lives…that is a time when they need to be reached. I liked the name, I really did. (Well, I grew up in the lower Rio Grande VALLEY).

It was settled. (That is until about a year later when we found out people have trouble remembering more than three syllables. Sam made an executive decision and took the word "Creek" out of our name at that time.)

Now Bear (Creek) Valley Church could begin hunting members. We did not have to go far. In fact we did not have to really go anywhere and I was glad, since as you know, I do not like to go "out-there." We did not have to even "do" anything—to get our first member. In November of '91, my extended family had a gathering in the Galleria in Dallas, in what used to be El Fenix, down by the ice skating rink. My aunt and uncle from Tennessee were visiting my parents in East Texas and they were needing their Tex-Mex fix. The Galleria was kind of a central place for us to meet. We had asked my cousin, Audrey, and her little boy to join us. They lived in nearby Garland. In the course of the evening we shared our exciting news: we were starting a new church! Let me say here that upon hearing news of this sort, especially coming from a middle-aged couple who had been on "The Track" toward greatness, most people conveyed a mild skepticism about the venture. (Maybe I am too sensitive.) Everyone that evening, however, even my sixty-ish year old aunt and uncle applauded us for going for our dream. My own parents did, too, but they had had time to assimilate the knowledge.

While all my relatives that night were "all ears," it was my cousin, Audrey, who was the most interested in our plans. After hearing it, she said without hesitation, "I want to be a part. I don't care how far away it is in the Metroplex. I need it. I definitely want to be a part. Count me in. I am one of those unchurched people you are describing." Wow. On the way home that night Sam and I were excited. We could "be there" for Audrey, just by "being there." Her interest confirmed even more clearly that our new church was needed and that God was calling us here. And it meant we had our first core group member—my very own cousin, Audrey!

The excitement was building. God had indeed brought us here "for such a time as this."

With Northwood's consent we began looking around its congregation for more core group members. A core group, it should be stated, is a group that would meet several months before the start-date, to pray and plan how this new church would work.

The first thing we did was to hold a Sunday afternoon meeting in the sanctuary of Northwood Church. That was in November of 1991. There Sam and I shared our dream of a new church. I sang the song I had just finished, "What Can I Do?" The miracle of that song, as I have written earlier, was that I had composed the first part many years before, but couldn't complete it somehow. With the dream of Bear (Creek) Valley now in my head and heart, the Lord seemed to give me the rest of the song. After I sang it, Sam presented the vision for Bear (Creek) Valley. It would be designed, he said, to reach the unchurched. If anyone was interested in knowing more about what we were doing and being a part, they could talk to us afterwards.

The meeting ended and a few people came forward. Bill and Charlene Lewis were two of them. We liked them right away. We had known Bill slightly as he led the Royal Ambassadors at Northwood, a missions organization for young boys, of which our little Will was a part. Bill and Will seemed to hit it off from the start.

Bill and Charlene said they would like to be a part of the group that would help us get started. They would stay for six weeks and then resume their duties at Northwood. At the end of the six-week period we hoped to have our own people to do the work that the Northwood helpers had done. Besides Bill and Charlene to help us, about twenty-five people from our Sunday School class volunteered to spend those first six weeks with us. We are deeply indebted to them. Without their help where would we be now?

The Northwood volunteers gave selflessly those first few weeks, but no one more than Bill and Charlene Lewis. You can imagine the excitement Sam and I felt when after the six weeks were up Bill told us that he and Charlene, and their two kids, Shawn and Heather, felt compelled to stay on with Bear Valley as actual members! They had all prayed about it, and sensed God's strong leadership in that direction. Thank you, Lord! To say that was an answer to our prayers is an understatement.

The down-to-earth, fun Lewises started to become like family to the Carmacks. And as we were soon to learn, their family was far from typical.

Bill was reared in a Christian home. Somewhere along the way he strayed. He ended up in California one night beaten up from a motorcycle accident. He thought he might not even live through the night. He prayed for the first time in a long time. God, as He always does, heard the prayer. He answered that prayer by sending an unknown pastor by Bill's room to pray for him. Bill remembers the remarkable request…that his face would not be scarred… It was not, miraculously.

From that moment on he was back in the fold. He moved to his hometown, Lubbock, Texas, and proceeded to go back to church. It was there that he met a cute little single lady named Charlene. Charlene had a unique story of her own. She had been married but had no children. Her sister, a single mom with two young children, was brutally murdered leaving her children parentless. Charlene took over and became their mom. Unfortunately this didn't sit too well with Charlene's husband and he left her. When Bill met Charlene she was a struggling young divorcee with two little children to raise. Bill said, "I sensed that God was saying: This is the reason I have left you here on earth."

The rest is history…and we are a part of it. Hallelujah!

We've watched Shawn and Heather grow up.

The Lewises were on board for the long haul. They weren't the only Northwood members, though, to sign the dotted line. In that Northwood Sunday School class there was an impressive couple, Joe and Sheryl Forney. We learned they had been Peace Corps volunteers years earlier in Guatemala and I guess, with our Brazil experience, we felt an immediate connection. Sam began thinking and praying about approaching them to help us start our church. After feeling God's go-ahead we met with them and presented the idea. They were for it...all six of them, Joe, Sheryl, and their children, Matthew, Rebecca, Nathan and three-year-old Andrew.

We were off! The living room lobby of our apartment complex, the Arbors at Central Park in Bedford, became the Monday night meeting place for our core group, starting in January, 1992. Initially it was Audrey, Bill and Charlene, Joe and Sheryl, and Sam and I that met. Our next-door neighbors, Cindy Burnham and her husband David, and their friend, Tracy Legge, a single mom, joined soon after. Then Pam and Ken. This was a great mix of Christians, non-Christians, churched and unchurched. While the adults were meeting, little Will and Laura, ages six and four, would stay with a sitter that we found through the apartment manager.

After much searching Sam found the General Cinema at Central Park in Bedford to be our Bear Creek Valley Church meeting place. Easter, April 19, 1992 was set as our launch date, with the Sunday before being a dress rehearsal. From January to April Sam was busy designing a mailer that would be sent to 40,000 residents from Euless to Hurst. He also bought a trailer from C&S that our mini van could pull. He parked the trailer in a storage rental place off of Hwy 183 in Euless. In the trailer we put all kinds of sound equipment, lighting equipment, coffee pots, tables, rocking chairs, portable baby beds, etc., etc. It's my opinion that the average church member of the average church has no idea what goes into "putting on church." That is, until he finds himself having to get all the equipment for it and making room in a trailer for all that equipment. I guess the saying, "Ignorance is bliss" might apply here. I had never dreamed what it would take to "do church." I was getting an education fast. We all were. No one more than Sam...and yet, in spite of all the work, he seemed invincible. Maybe it was BECAUSE of all the work.

If you start a church expect to work very hard for the first five years. Each week is like running wind sprints and not marathons.

In our core meetings we began to determine just where everyone would serve. Sam would do basically everything—except what he absolutely couldn't. He would get the trailer and the donuts on Sunday morning...with Will, Laura and me helping with the donuts. (I'll tell more about that later.)

I would be the music director, since I could play the piano and sing. I was eager to teach those snazzy choruses we had learned the previous summer out in California. It was understood, of course, that we would use our huge Kurzweil keyboard (the same kind Stevie Wonder played, I'll have you know). This went without question until we realized that each and every Sunday we'd have to get two big strong men (one would be Sam, of course) to carry it down from our third-story bedroom from our upper two-story apartment. Somehow that made all the equipment in the trailer look like featherweights. Ah, but it was for a fantastic cause.

It was determined that I needed a kind of choir, an ensemble, if you will, to help me get the audience singing. Cindy (our next door neighbor) and Tracey (her friend from two apartments away) said they really liked to sing and wanted to give it a try. One afternoon the three of us met in our bedroom to practice. It was then that I realized just how little church experience these two precious ladies had had. I began playing the hymn, "Amazing Grace." My thinking was that we needed to have some music that the visitors would know. As I began playing and singing I noticed they were not joining in. "Come on. Let me hear you sing."

"We don't know this song," Cindy said.

Tracey chimed in, "Well, I think I've heard it before. I think it was in the movie *Silkwood*."

I tried not to let them see my mouth hanging open.

What a lesson that was to me. Never assume knowledge. Just because something in the Christian life has been with you since birth, don't assume the average person knows about it…because it's likely that they do not.

It was my joy to teach those gals that beautiful old hymn. Needless to say, I sing it now with much more feeling than I used to.

As a side note, those two ladies were among the first group we baptized at Bear Valley a few months later.

What do you think about non-believers helping put on a worship service? This is a pretty controversial issue with good reason. We wanted to involve people before they made a commitment to Christ. Some call this pre-discipleship. I think of it being what Jesus did for his followers. I believe the key to urban evangelism is learning to create real community with non-believers. Eventually, here is what we came up with (I hope you can improve on it): A curious, non-believer could help, even on the stage, if there is nothing in his life which would cause embar-

rassment to the church; however, when it came to articulating the message, we insisted that he believe the essentials of the faith and is on a membership-track. Everything else, such as ushering, sound engineering, and many other spots, are open to anyone who is curious about the faith. Because of this approach, we have led several musicians to Christ. Similarly I have had several extended conversations about Christ as we would load the trailer.

I'm getting carried away with the music aspect of Bear Valley. I will get carried away again, but for now let me get back on task. I was writing about how each member of the core group was given a task, as we looked forward to the first service of Bear Creek Valley Church. We needed a soundman and a light man. It turned out to be the same man! For the first six weeks of the church it was Audrey's sometimes-estranged husband, Jerry. Off and on it would also be Joe Forney or David Burnham, or young Shawn Lewis, who at around fourteen was quite the helper. He would do anything you would ask of him. I wanted young Will to take notice!

One of the benefits of church planting—perhaps the best benefit—is the family connection. There used to be a time in our culture when families would work together, the family farm or business. That has almost completely disappeared today. One major exception is starting a church. My best memories are connected to doing this with my family.

The most important part of the church, next to music, of course, would be the children's area. I believe working with children is the most thankless job. Oh, parents can often be grateful, but really never quite enough.

Supervising lots of children at one time is more work than most people can imagine. I'm, of course, speaking from experience. Back in the days when I would take a turn at helping out in preschool Sunday School classes, I would vow never to do it again, unless it involved lots of money. 'Course my tongue is right in the middle of my cheek just now. Seriously, children's work is so underrated. That's why I want to laud Sheryl Forney and Charlene Lewis for all the work they did those first months and years at Bear Valley. As far as I am concerned, they couldn't have gotten enough money for what they did. Oh, and Bill Lewis, was—for years and years—the elementary school age teacher. It was decided that we would show Christian children's videos for the school age children as their Sunday School. After hearing a children's sermon by Sam, Mr. Bill would escort them to another theater where they would watch a video on the big screen. Bill, Sheryl and Charlene's work would not only be plentiful, but it would also mean that they could never attend an adult worship service. Their love and sacrifice will never be forgotten.

So we had the preacher, the music leader, the sound and light man, the children's workers, the helpers from Northwood who were mainly greeters, and family members of all those just listed to help us set up and tear down our new church. The General Cinema at Central Park was a really nice facility. It was new and modern and very clean. The management was very helpful and seemed excited that a church was going to meet there.

We were ready. We set April 19, 1992 (Easter) as our first public Sunday with the week before that as a "dress rehearsal." The week before the dress rehearsal we took all the sound and light equipment to Northwood and set it up to see if it worked. It did. We were in business!

Palm Sunday became our Dress Rehearsal. And it was a good thing we had it, because that dress rehearsal service lasted only ten minutes, because it took longer than expected to set up all the equipment! (In another venue the service could have lasted longer, but since the movie theater was going to start showing movies at a certain time, well, we had to be out of there before the previews started!)

The night before April 19, I don't think either Sam or I slept much. As the song goes, "anticipation was making us wait." How many would show up? 10 or 1000? We'd sent out thousands of mailers and we knew that according to those in the know, less than one percent responds to impersonal mailers. I surely never respond to mailers. The trashcan is the file I put them in. Needless to say, much prayer was shot up, asking God to have those people looking carefully at their mail and to draw them to our flyer.

If it hasn't been said before it needs to be said now that Bear Valley was the very first "from scratch" seeker-type church in the Fort Worth area. One had been started in Dallas a year or two earlier. (The term "seeker church" was used at that time to describe these new-fangled untraditional churches.)

Easter is sometimes cold around North Texas. This really dampens the spirits of the feminine gender who have picked our their Easter parade outfits and white shoes to announce the spring/summer wardrobe change. Of course one of our high values—and that we advertised in our mailer—was our casual dress code for Bear Creek Valley Church. The Easter parade would be toned down a bit, but surely it would not be canceled. At least for me. Ah, but the chilly weather did hamper my showing off as I wanted to: I had to bring a sweater that would cover up my new short-sleeved blouse. Little did I know until I woke up that morning that I would need a raincoat as well. Rats. Not only would my new clothes be completely covered up, but also new people might not show up. As we have found in church work, any change in the weather brings many excuses for staying home from church, even on Easter.

How many came? We counted exactly 100 people! We were delighted. Thrilled. There were children in the children's area—babies and preschoolers in the hallways of the theaters, and school age children in one of the smaller theaters. Adults were in the largest theater, where most of the sound system and all of the lighting worked!

It was a great start. The only big blunder—on our part, anyway—was our wrong estimation of how many donuts came in the donut boxes we had bought at Sam's Wholesale Club the day before. I'm not sure how many boxes we bought, but it was A LOT. Well, with one dozen donuts in a box, we could maybe serve ten people. Some would eat one, some none, and some two or more. Too bad no one was super hungry that morning…since each box had not just one dozen but TWO dozen donuts in it! After church we were standing outside giving entire boxes of donuts to all those new attenders. When was the last time you visited church and instead of a welcome card, they gave you a box of donuts? Even with giving them away we still had leftover boxes. We found out that you can freeze them, but once thawed they're not something you'd want to serve if you were trying to impress. (Some garbage diggers had their sugar fix that week.)

That first service is remembered fondly. Watching the people show up made our hearts swell. No one was late as I recall. As with every important thing anyone does, there is usually Murphy's Law to contend with: as the service was getting ready to start, Sam plugged in the lapel microphone and the sound system went dead. Fortunately the system came back to life, but he didn't think he could use his lapel mic. When it came time for the message titled "Never Fear Failure," he spoke loudly and told the story of the mic. Then he asked, "What do you think? Should I risk plugging in the mic?" "Yes!" was the crowd's reply. He did, and it worked! Prior to that point in the service we all thought he would just have to yell the sermon out that day.

This moment became a metaphor at Bear Valley for taking big risks for God.

To start the service I sang an opener-solo, then Sam (with a booming voice) welcomed everyone, congratulating them on being the first attenders of this brand new kind of church in the Metroplex. I then led the new church in singing a few choruses, while playing the big Kurzweil keyboard.

After the group singing Sam had everyone turn and greet each other. I could see everyone in the theater, so I saw the greeting that a well-dressed, handsome, middle-aged couple gave each other—a kiss. It brought a smile to my face. We later came to know and love this couple, Ted and Nanci Freemon, but during the first few weeks of the church, I just thought of them as the couple that kissed each other during the greeting time.

Now as everyone knows the real test of a successful church start is not how many people come to the first service, but how many come back the next Sunday!! The night before that Sunday was probably our most awake night of all. Ah, but the next morning proved to be great. We had about eighty people. Most were returns, some were brand new. We were feeling pretty good. We only had a few extra donuts that day.

I would be remiss to fail to mention that this approach is not the best way to start a church. Today I would use a preview method, where you preview your worship event once a month for four to six months. This allows you to focus on building a larger core group without having to produce a quality service every week. Also it is easier to borrow great musicians from another church for one service, but back to the story...

During the first week of the church, Sam got a phone call that threw him for a loop. The fire marshal of Bedford was calling. He'd heard that we were starting a church in the cinema and that was a problem. Bedford had strict rules on who could meet where. Since the General Cinema at Central Park was not zoned for a church, we had to be out. Out! Incredible. We had sent out thousands of mailers saying we were meeting in at the Bedford cinema. Were we supposed to send out thousands more mailers telling the people, "Oops, just kidding." Seriously, though, this was disastrous, with weeks away from summer.

Where were we to go...and when? After much pleading, the city gave us a month to be out. Four weeks. Sam was very disappointed. Where do we go? He looked around and found...the mall! Northeast Mall in Hurst had a cinema that would take us. This was good news because Northeast Mall was extremely well known in the area. This was bad news, though, because Northeast Mall Cinema was old and in need of repair. Of course the worst part of it was having to get the word out that we were moving. That would take time, and lots of money. But what else could we do but move? On a side note, let me say that five years later Bear Valley sponsored a church, CenterPoint, that did begin meeting in that same Central Cinema in Bedford. Its pastor, Jay Bruner, knew from our experience, to talk with the city and obtain a special waver. Though we moved to a dirtier, older theater, it turned out to be just the right place for us at that time. (Ah, but we didn't know that for a while.)

Most of the people who came to the first location did NOT follow us to the Northeast Mall cinema. In essence, we had to restart the church the next fall.

Well, summer is always hard on churches. People take vacations which means they don't come to services and they don't give their money when they don't come. We were getting ready to find out how hard summers are on church-starts. Because of this finding, Sam now encourages young church planters to NOT start on Easter, particularly if Easter falls late in the spring. April 19 was a pretty late Easter. Summer was looking dismal.

On the weekend of June 2, 1992 we had planned a 50th wedding anniversary for Sam's parents. That was very fortunate. Sam's sister and her family, and brother and his family came to the metroplex and celebrated. They all attended Bear Valley that Sunday. If they had not we would have been very depressed. About thirty-two people were in church that day. Fourteen were Carmacks. You do the math…and see the "dismalness." Of course, it was all about quality, we would tell ourselves.

I should say here that with this dismal attendance Sam was beginning to worry. He did not want to lose the core members we had but thought that the size of the church might be a real downer for them and they might bail. What a surprise: As he talked with them, one by one, he found that all of the people who were new to church could care less about the crowd-size. They were having a ball, as they were—for the first time—experiencing a church just for them. Only the churchgoers were concerned.

And that Carmack fiftieth anniversary weekend was great for them—it got to show Sam's family how much fun this "teeny tiny" church was.

I want to say a word here about the Carmack family and their support of our church start. From day one Bob and Oleta (Sam's parents) were excited. They always had a missionary spirit. During Sam's childhood he remembers many a missionary that would stay in his home while there to speak at First Baptist Church, Hinton, Oklahoma. Through the years as Bob and Oleta would travel the world they would have missionaries show them their work. When Bob and Oleta would come home they would pray about where to send money. Then send it they would…to Kenya to help build an orphanage…to Thailand to help put roofs on new church buildings…wherever they saw a need, they would try and help meet it.

They even funded groups of seminary students to take mission trips, most notably to the Canary Islands, and to the Yucatan Peninsula in Mexico. When Sam and I went to Brazil as missionaries we found that many of the missionary parents were filled with anxiety and loss when their children went overseas. Understandably so...but not for Nana and Daddy Bob. They were our staunchest supporters. Their hearts were always in missions. So when we shared with them the news that we wanted to start a church for the unchurched, the first thing they said was, "How can we help?" The first thing they did, of course, was to let us move in with them for as long as it would take to figure out where to go and what to do. They were also helpful financially. We couldn't have started the church without them, actually. A portion of the $38,000 that we needed and used at the beginning was from their generous gift-giving. In fact it was their gift that meant we could have a video projector.

After the "sing-togethers" in the worship service, Shawn would roll the projector into the elementary area for Bill to use to show animated Christian videos to the children. Now, obviously, the early church back in the first century was started without a video projector. The mind boggles at how fast it might have grown if it had had one. In a dark theater, though, a good video projector is a must.

Sam's brother and sister were also helpful. In fact, through the years their gifts and offerings have proved to be one of the reasons for Bear Valley's success. Examples: The Rosses, Ken and Pat (Sam's sis), gave a high-end projector as well as the very best coffee maker money could buy when Ken's law office bought new ones, which then became the best, of course. Steve, Sam's brother, ended up buying some video editing equipment for the church. He was just giving what the Lord laid on his heart to give. As it happened, Sam had picked out two methods to edit video. One cost $2,000 and the other, much better, cost $12,000. Sam remembers praying, "Lord, we'll only go with the more expensive route if You miraculously supply the money." Soon after that prayer we were at a Carmack family gathering and Steve slipped a check into Sam's pocket. The amount: $12,000. (It will be told later how Steve gave more personally, but that is a different chapter.)

Steve and Ken also helped out by bringing personal testimonies to our Sunday services. One day Steve shared about the pain of his divorce and how God saw him through it. Another Sunday Ken told of how God is faithful and true in the world of practicing law. (That got a lot of attention, like an oxymoron does.) (Ken bears the brunt of our lawyer jokes.)

There is something to be said for quality, not quantity. That summer some of the cream of the crop found Bear Valley and we're glad we found them: Greg and Laurie Bargsley with their little Alex and infant Ian. Our son, Will, made a lasting friend in Alex as the months turned into years. Laurie turned out to be a great promoter of the church. She told a fellow teacher who told a friend who came and gave our daughter, Laura, one of her best friends through the years. Jay Gosdin had told his wife he would go to church if she found one that had good, rock music, where you could dress casually, and where the schedule would not conflict with the Dallas Cowboy football games (many churches held services on Sunday evenings). He had other criteria, I'm sure, and it was all in an attempt to get his precious wife off his back. He actually made a list. Martha had wanted the family to start going to church together. Jay had other plans. That was until Laurie Bargsley told Marilyn Duncan who told Martha Gosdin about Bear Valley.

Then there were Robert and Peggy Werner and son, toddler Gregory. This was an interesting family. He's a devout Aggie and an airline pilot and she, an Aggie as well, is half Japanese and half Chinese. Their family has expanded to five, adding Benjamin and Aubrey. Through the years the Werners have been stalwarts of the Bear Valley clan.

Then there's Dine´ Lewis, a tall, beautiful black lady. Interesting story here. It seems that she attended before she actually attended. Her first week she drove up and parked in the mall parking lot...staying in her car. She was checking out who was attending this new-fangled church, to see if she would fit in. When she did start coming into the building she sat in the back. Anonymous. Well, fast forward: she became an integral part of the church and eventually became our drama director! Dine´ was raised in New York and had made her way to Texas as an adult because of a business venture. Her nonSouthern ways have helped us in reaching more folks with her background. Unfortunately a diagnosis of Multiple Sclerosis several years ago has curtailed much of her activity.

And there were the Morrisons, Patrick and Louise. They came to Bear Valley after receiving one of our mailers—and have been members ever since. Patrick has had major heart problems, which have kept him home, but Louise has been one of our most regular members. She also has brought three of their grandchildren, which they have been raising, becoming their legal guardians since they've been at Bear Valley. We have watched Josie, Jonathan and little Christopher grow up before our eyes.

Oh, and there were Chuck and Mary Kratz. Wonderful couple. He became our treasurer and a helper in setting up and tearing down. She became the proofreader for our bulletins (programs) each week. We loved them. One of the saddest times was when I heard they were leaving to go back to their roots—the kind of church in which they grew up.

We found that one of the purposes of Bear Valley has been to get people back in church. Unfortunately that means that some return to the church of their childhood and leave Bear Valley. I say "unfortunately" because it is our loss, but in the overall scheme of this—God's world—it is indeed wonderful that people like Chuck and Mary have returned to their "first love."

Being in a theater that is part of a mall has its advantages. One of them was Bob Elliott, an elderly gentleman who routinely walked the mall early Sunday mornings. One Sunday his curiosity got the better of him and he had to check us out. We were needing someone of his generation, to add stability to our fold. He became a part and we found that the more we got to know him, the more we were impressed. We found out that he engineered the first remote control for model airplanes. Bob's popularity in our church was evident the night we had his 70th birthday party. Remember we were all closer to 30 than 70. A big turnout told him he had a big family. This was very good, because he had no family of his own, and until recently had lived by himself.

I cannot make a list of Bear Valley movie theater folks without mentioning Bob and Barbara Daniels in whose pool we had our first baptism. We also held our first 101 class there (membership class). Our first small group meeting was held in the home of Ted and Nanci Freemon. Sam led a study of "Who is Jesus?" It was a hit. In fact, everyone in it, about twelve people, were soon baptized. Sam says one of his best moments was the night he began to teach that group to pray. He simply had them go around the circle and tell God something they appreciated. How exciting to hear those prayers! The next small group meetings were held in the home of Butch and Marti Potvin. Butch was almost like a staff member. He knew all about small groups and helped us a lot. Many of these families have moved on but without their help we would not be what we are today. God brought them along just for us—just for then.

I don't want to forget the Holmes family. Ken, Penny, Jennifer, Andrya, and Ryan got a mailer and, as I recall, the fact that this was a casual church was what impressed them. They wanted to get into a church, and the idea of not having to go buy "church clothes," was a major selling point. Remember, this was 1992 when churches were still pretty formal. That family has played a major role in our church, and as I write, Penny is now the Bear Valley Drama Director.

In those early days we became "family" with so many: the Buchanans, the Bowdens, and the Prathers and the Bobos (of whom I'll write more later), besides many, many more. I wish I could tell every story…and maybe someday I will.

God had been leading us each step of the way. That's not to mean that I was the perfect "truster" of his guidance. No. You'd think, with all this fun, and all these fun new folks, I would be going around singing God's praises all the time. Oh, I did, but not all the time. I do so remember loving those days. And yet, I remember my rebellious ways—even if they were mainly in my head. And that's where they were, frequently, the first few months of the church. As I said, that first summer our attendance was very small. My eyes were looking at the quantity—because I didn't know at the time just how high the quality was. And in that summer of '92 my insomnia was back. One morning at around 4 a.m. I went down the stairs of our apartment to the kitchen and made some hot chocolate. No matter what time of year it is, I like hot chocolate in the wee morning hours. I got my journal out and began pouring my thoughts out onto it. I decided to get real with God and let him know that I didn't like being in this apartment and I didn't like starting this new-fangled church. And I didn't like my husband for doing this to me and I didn't like me for telling him I felt "led" to do it with him. In fact those "feeling led" moments were so emotional I was disgusted with myself for succumbing to them. I was thinking how God plays a number on us when he gets us all worked up and then—like that wee-morning-hour—we're faced with the choices we made when our emotions were strong. Ah, so I was mad at God, too, for making me "feel led" to do this crazy church thing. Yes, He IS ultimately responsible, anyway.

The main focus that early hour though, was not God, or Sam, but me, myself and I. Often through the years I have had a running war with self-dislike. I would say "self-hate," but I don't think it was that strong. The older I get the more I see that self-hate is a common malady in women. That, of course, is the subject of another book maybe I'll write someday. For that early morning hour, though, I was immersed in negativity. I didn't like myself and was feeling far from God, whom I was not liking at the moment. I sat there wallowing in self-pity. I thought I'd just be still for a while and enjoy the quiet. After a few moments of stillness, I felt a profound peace come over me. I grabbed my pen and began to write. A few times in my life I have sensed God speaking to me in this way. It's not a voice I hear, or writing on the wall. It is just a sense that He is telling me something. In my journals I have labeled it HTM (He Tells Me). Usually it happens when I stop and listen with my heart to what I think He wants me to know. This early morning, though, I really wasn't seeking Him. I was just being quiet, after some ranting and raving about how much I didn't like my lot in life at that moment and how much I didn't like myself either. I wanted to work through this self-disgust, but thought I would just end up writing some affirmations, etc., to help me feel better. I really didn't expect the Almighty to give me a message. He did. I found myself writing, "Nancy, I love you truly, completely and forever." That was all I wrote, but it was as if the world stood still. I looked at those words and somehow felt the arms of God hugging me. It's hard to explain. It was a peace that definitely passed understanding. And it continues to pass understanding. Often, since that morning, I have recalled how

God hugged me and told me He loved me. It has carried me many a morning since then. I have done a little study on the words, "truly," "completely" and "forever" and have seen how that just about covers God's love for me. Just writing about it now is almost overwhelming.

Oh yes, I survived the summer of '92 gloriously. Knowing in my gut that God loved me truly, completely and forever made all the set up and tear down of our church at Northeast Mall's cinema worth it.

Well, there is one thing I really didn't like—but God's love made it worth it. It was making that Tang drink in the kitchen of the movie theater concession stand each and every Sunday morning.

It was my own fault—that job of making the fake orange juice. I had been feeling for the children and adults who did not drink coffee. That had been the only beverage we offered with our donuts. Surely we should have orange juice or something. Well, having fresh orange juice every week would be a challenge because we certainly couldn't keep it in the trailer during the week. It would be wasteful to buy OJ and pour out what wasn't drunk each week. The solution I came up with: Tang! What a great idea. When we purchased the big coffee bags from Sam's Wholesale Club, we'd just purchase a big can of Tang. We bought a large water cooler-thing and we were in business. Actually, I thought someone else might DO the business of making the Tang. Alas, no one volunteered. Since it was my idea, and I made the coffee anyway, I was the natural Tang maker. I never minded too much making that coffee but the fake orange juice became another issue. Many-a-time I would have an orange arm. Somehow the spoon used to stir the Tang was just not long enough. I don't think I need any more description. Needless to say, when we moved to our next location we quit offering the orange beverage. We would have quit sooner, but you know it is hard to stop serving something that children like. Yes, they actually liked it. Ah, but I used to like it, too, when it came out in the sixties as astronaut juice.

Tang provides a very good lesson. Consistency is extremely important. Why do I go to McDonalds when I travel? There are better hamburgers. It's because I know I will always get the same quality wherever. Be careful what you start, because it will do damage when you stop it. Just about any change creates negative momentum.

chapter 6

The Band

> "So where does it get you, all this speaking in tongues no one understands? It doesn't help believers, and it only gives unbelievers something to gawk at... But if some unbelieving outsiders walk in on a service where people are speaking out God's truth, the plain words will bring them up against the truth and probe their hearts. Before you know it, they're going to be on their faces before God, recognizing that God is among you." (1 Corinthians 14:22–25 Message)

Before Nancy tells you about The Band, here are a few principles concerning music in a church start. Of course you always want the best music possible, but when the church is small you have to find a way to do it with volunteers. I was fortunate. My wife sang like Karen Carpenter and played the keyboard like Richard; but even that becomes monotonous. We figured out that it is cheaper to hire band members than music leaders. The term used today is, use contract players instead of employees as much as you can. Fortunately, I knew enough about music to oversee it. Here's a principle: You add an employee when you need to add management. Contract talent, employ management. During the first year, my biggest challenge was figuring out how to help Nancy feel comfortable working with professional musicians. Remember the idea: helping each other with life goals. That's been a big part of my job—helping Nancy to find a way to share her music. Check out www.nancycarmack.com. I hope to have some of her music available.

To say that making Tang was all I didn't like would be lying. God's love is good, though, and realizing it can make even scary things manageable. Like playing with a band. When we started the church, I was the sole musician. I played the keyboard (adding an easy-to-use drum machine a little later) and sang the choruses extra loud so all could sing along with me. Sam likes to say, "most church planters start a service that is sensitive to seekers. We started a piano bar that was sensitive to Christians." That playing and singing worked fine for me. Even with Cindy and Tracey as my ensemble singers, it worked fine. In fact, with just Sam and me doing the services we could still be planning the order of songs, etc., as we lay in bed on Saturday night. Well, that mom and pop show did not last forever.

One day Sam approached me with the idea of bringing on a drummer and a bass guitar player. Instead of me being the sole band, it would be a trio of musicians. One would think I would have jumped for joy. Wrong. I started to cry. To explain those tears would take a treatise beginning with how I wished I had taken music theory more seriously as a youngster. Really. All my insecurities as a musician were surfacing. I knew that not only was I weak in music theory but, since I was never in a school band or a choir that was worth anything, I had trouble counting and keeping up with the beat of the director. Well, I'd never had a director period. When I was in the fifth grade, after two years of piano lessons, my teacher began to cry telling me I would never amount to much of a pianist if I did not learn to count well. Unfortunately, I took seven more years of lessons (with a different teacher, by the way), and never did heed that teacher's advice as I should have. Well, now I was doing the crying. Oh, I could lead a group singing choruses as long as I was the only one who was playing the instrument. It's easy to follow myself…or lead myself. Keeping up with a drummer and a bass player was going to be more of a challenge than I was really wanting. The fact that where Sam was going to start looking for the drummer and bass player was at The University of North Texas' world famous music/jazz school, did not help me with my insecurities, not one iota. I knew, however, that our new church would be changing and improving as time went on. One of those improvements had to come in the area of music. The adage "No pain, No gain," could fit here. Today, I can look back and say that it was well worth my discomfort to pursue musical excellence. Not only was our music going to be enhanced, but also my own musical skill would be profoundly affected for the better. My old music teacher would be proud. Yes, I found myself learning to count in spite of myself.

Here's a note for piano players. Playing keyboard in a rock band is very different from playing the piano. The change is not real hard, if you know chords.

Now finding that first drummer and bass player shouldn't be too hard, we reasoned. We were thirty minutes from the premier jazz music school in the world,

University of North Texas. Surely there would be some students there who would jump at the chance to play for a pittance. We wanted to get professional musicians (though not expensive ones) from day one (with the exception of myself) so that our quality of music would appeal to an unchurched seeker.

Here's an interesting fact. Generally, the Christian is more concerned about the quality of music than the seeker. The seeker is more concerned about the message, primarily the ability to take away something meaningful and practical every week. The music for the seeker becomes an issue of credibility. Does the music add a level of credibility? That is, is it "professional?" This will be measured by the culture you are reaching. A Cowboy church will have a different criteria of professionalism than a suburban church in N.E. Tarrant County. An addition of a professional guitarist probably didn't impress many Christians, but it would speak volumes to the religiously curious. We need to do a lot more thinking about how the arts help reach our culture. Unfortunately, most churches never get beyond worrying about how music keeps their members content.

Sam put up an ad on the University of North Texas Baptist Student Center bulletin board and waited. Sure enough, calls started coming. The first young man who came and auditioned was very much in my realm of ability. It would be like the blind leading the blind. Fortunately he could tell right away that we were needing someone with more skill in playing in a band. We didn't have to turn him down, he turned us down. The next young man who came to our house for an interview and audition was a big, burly, ponytailed fella named Pete

Wagstaff. The interview was so-so, but the minute he began playing his bass guitar, Sam and I looked at each other and nodded, "oh yes." Pete brought his drummer-friend, John Pollard, over a few nights later and that was the beginning of the Bear Valley Band. The three of us would practice every Wednesday night in our dining room, getting ready for the following Sunday.

Though the work involved got tedious, we found that a dark theater afforded anonymity that so many of the radically unchurched want and even need. They can almost hide in there, which makes for a safe way to consider God's truths. No pretense, no defense, just sitting in the dark, absorbing God's love. A very common response to this was crying. That seemed so odd, what with the services being upbeat and fun, and these new people crying. Then Sam and I realized that many of these folks, who had not been in church in years, had responded to our mailers because they were hurting and needing healing. The dark auditorium was such a safe place for them to let themselves feel and heal. Even in a room with lots of empty seats, no one really sticks out.

There were many, many services with lots of empty seats. Until, that is, the Bill Bates day. To reach more people for Christ, Sam decided to use a Rick Warren idea of having a celebrity come speak. Mailers with free Bible coupons would be sent advertising the big event and hopefully people would come. Sam was right on target. I, personally, didn't know the name Bill Bates from a stranger's name on the street, but a lot of Dallas Cowboy fans did. The largest auditorium at Northeast Mall Cinema was packed that day. Talk about thrilling. Bill Bates gave a wonderful testimony of how he trusted in God on the football field and off. It was fantastic. His talk was only outdone by his wonderful, kind manner off-stage. To this day, when people tell how they came to Christ at Bear Valley, many will point to that day when they came to hear Cowboy Bill Bates.

Others point to the day we had Cowboy Jim Jeffcoat, who came and spoke a few months later.

Try to budget for celebrities. Yes, many of them do free appearances, but that list is very long. To get on the short list, you need to pay. If it is supplementing your advertising, it usually is a good use of money. Fortunately, they don't charge churches as much as a business.

When they do come only give them about twenty minutes to speak. You want your guests to see enough of the regular service to see that they might like coming back. When we had a celebrity we would introduce a new series, which would interest even a non-Christian, or at least promote the topic for the next three weeks. These principles apply to any high attendance Sunday, such as Easter.

Our overall attendance began climbing slowly since the Bill Bates and Jim Jeffcoat days. Because of Bill and Jim our average attendance went over 100. This is a very hard number to pass for churches starting slowly like ours. To make it climb even higher we decided to send out another mailer. Now creating a good mailer takes quite a bit of marketing skill, which I would have to say, Sam has developed. We found, however, that no matter how sharp the mailer looks if it doesn't have all the information needed, it really may be not very effective. I pride myself in what a good proofreader I am. Through the years I have proofread everything that Sam has written, from letters, to program notes, to even his Ph.D. dissertation. I can catch many a typo. Unfortunately, I did not catch the error in our second big mailer, for Mother's Day 1992. The place of our church was in big letters (NorthEast Mall), the topic of the upcoming sermons was in big letters, the dates of those topics were in big letters. The only thing that was not in big or even small letters was the time of our service! What a glaring mistake!

A few people called and asked about the time, others just stayed home. I'm sure they would have come in droves if we had put the time of the service on that mailer. (It's nice to have a good excuse for poor attendance every now and then.)

Most of the time while we were having church in the NorthEast Mall movie theater, Sam had his church office in our home. In the apartment he put a desk and some bookcases in the third bedroom and called it his study. Will and Laura were little then and didn't mind sharing a bedroom. When we moved to our home in Grapevine, he declared the living room area his office. That was fine with me. Will and Laura each had their own room, and we had a spacious den so we didn't need a living room. We knew there would come a time when we'd need office space with more than one room. I was kind of enjoying this business of starting a church from scratch, and even having my husband working at home most of the time. Anybody else working in our home with Sam, other than me, though, would not make me a happy church-starter's wife.

This brings up the subject of minister's houses. In our denomination we call the pastor's house "the parsonage." Down through the years the church parsonage has often been located close to the church. In Chattanooga, Oklahoma, it was across the parking lot and it was of the same brick as the church building. Everybody knew where the pastor and his family lived. That can be a good thing for the congregation. They know they always have access to the pastor, and they know if he's not in his office, he's just across the way, at home. Many folks would just come over at any time and want to talk about church stuff. A better pastor's wife would have been glad to put on a pot of coffee and let them have at it. Well, I might have put on the pot of coffee, but it would be inside my head that there would be fuming. Privacy, I want my privacy!!!

When we moved to Kentucky, the church had a parsonage but it was several blocks from the church building. I liked that a lot. We didn't get the constant stream of church members coming through our home. 'Course in both places we had church members who would delight in telling me how previous pastor's wives had decorated the living room, dining room or whatever…and how crazy they thought it was that a certain wall paper was chosen, etc., etc. One lady told me she was aghast at how dirty the master bathroom shower stall was when the former pastor's family moved out. Of course that made me keep the shower stall super clean. Still, what would be my flaw in homemaking that would be talked about when we left? I hated to think.

Well, so now, in the Metroplex, we (gladly) didn't live in a parsonage but had our own place…to call our own. And even if we did have the church office in the living room, and the music rehearsal in the dining room, and the small group meetings in the den, oh, and some staff meetings in the kitchen, well, it was OUR kitchen.

Speaking of staff members, our very first was Larry McCrary, a Southwestern Baptist Theological Seminary student. He was content to work in his home, but occasionally would come for meetings with Sam and me in our den. Larry was really considered an intern, as he was paid—if at all—very little. He, his wife, Susan, and daughter, Megan, are shown in a picture at the Northeast Mall that was part of an article in the Fort Worth STAR TELEGRAM in 1992. Our church was so unique that it made the news!

Actually, what caught the attention of the reporter was our use of a Free Bible Coupon in our mailer. As we gave Life Application Study Bibles, we enrolled new people in a Saturday afternoon conference at the Marriott Courtyard called, "Introduction to the Life Application Bible." At the end of that session, we gave them a chance to sign up for a "Who Is Jesus?" small group lasting only six weeks. We baptized twelve people from that group and discovered two key core group members for the future.

Larry went on to start several churches and eventually became a church-planting strategist for the Southern Baptist North American Mission Board. (This was very exciting for us as one of our goals was to develop many likeminded church planters.)

Our first really official staff member (not an intern) was Tim Bobo. Fortunately, he also was able to office at his own home. Tim became Sam's right-hand man. We decided it would be good to have weekly staff meetings, with Sam, Tim, and me, and the logical place to have it was at our breakfast table. Some days Tim would bring his precious little toddler, Katie, who would just play by herself as the nitty gritty work of Bear Valley was carried on by Sam and Tim.

Tim was Bear Valley's associate pastor at about the time that Judie Miller became Bear Valley's chef, and hostess with the mostest! It was not a paid position, but Judie and her husband Jimmy, would have the monthly 101 and 201 classes in their home for a while, and Judie would serve her famous lasagna, or some other homemade deliciousness for supper.

This was so great that Judie was our hostess. Though I like having meetings in my house sometimes, the idea of serving food at meetings sometimes stresses me out. Well, if I'm expected to cook that food, that is. I just have never considered myself the hostess with the mostest. Thankfully, Judie took that job!!!

After a while, with more folks getting involved, and activities going on, it was becoming clear that we needed office space and a conference room or two. Sam went on the lookout. Near Central and 183, on the north side, he found just the place. It even had a little kitchen. We were excited. A lot happened there besides business. We had at least two Super Bowl parties, plus some of our 101 and 201 classes (they were more fun in the Millers' home, though). I also started a Tuesday night equivalent of Sunday School for our kids. We called it Bear Club and it was fun! We (they) learned about the Bible by playing games, and singing songs. Our main attenders were Will, Laura, Marcie Gosdin, Josie Morrison, Alex Bargsley and his neighbors Krystal and Courtney Horst. Also Jesse and Molly Prather came on board (I'll tell more about them later). Martha Gosdin was my main helper. We kept Bear Club going for quite a while—well, until the church could have its own full-fledged children's program, and not just watch Bible videos on Sunday, while the adults attended "big church."

I did Bear Club as mainly a selfish thing. I knew my own children needed to learn about the Bible more, and well, somehow I wasn't doing what some parents wonderfully do at home: have family time—with Scripture memory, and character-building lessons—so, I thought, maybe if I make it a "class," then I will discipline myself to teach them about God and Jesus that way. And other kids could benefit, too.

So that's what we did…and we started it at that office space on Central.

It was at that office space on Central that we got to know the Prathers. You know the kind of people—the kind that you get so close to that you think they should be at your family reunions! Really.

The Prathers attended church in the movie theater. Somehow they found out about our church-start and wanted to check it out. We had mutual friends, and we'd heard that Keith had a killer voice, and could do some good guitar work, as well as keyboard work. Well, we had him sing a solo in the movie theater, and we were blown away. Whoa. We wanted him on board. But it was not until our Super Bowl party at the office space on Central that we got acquainted with the whole family. You talk about a darling family. Keith and Susan were fun personified (no wonder we got to know them at a party). They passed that fun trait down to their cute kids, Jesse and Molly. Jesse and Molly became fast friends with Will and Laura. Eventually Keith became our worship leader, while Susan became active on the music team. She learned to sing solos and sang many, but her love was, as she called it, being the "doo-wop" girl, singing backup to anyone anytime.

They were an integral part of Bear Valley for years. We couldn't afford to give Keith a full salary, so when his day job transferred him to Telluride, Colorado, well, we had to let them go. They were gone for seven long years. (They actually lived in Ridgeway, Colorado.) Now they're back, and using their gifts again at Bear Valley!

Well, back to talking about facilities. That dark, sticky-floored cinema at NorthEast Mall held lots of memories. And though it was not the ideal place to set up and tear down church, we only moved out of it because we had to. We had known from day one that it was old and worn out. Cinema management had realized that as well and informed us that renovation was starting soon. We had to be out in two months. Where would we go? In my meager mind, that presented some worry. Ah, but Sam has always loved a challenge. He got out and found some possible rental facilities. We even gathered the faithful and met at the darling shopping center on the southeast corner of Harwood and Hurstview in Hurst. I loved it. It had a great location and a wonderful feel. There was a cute little gazebo at the front corner and when we met to inspect it, that's where the children flocked to play. Too bad it was too expensive. Rats. Ah, but when God closes one door, thankfully He opens another one.

One day a realtor who specialized in church properties dropped by the church offices. Sam told him that we weren't interested in buying. As the realtor was about to leave, Sam asked, "By the way, do you know of anyone who would want to rent?" As a matter of fact…

On Davis Boulevard in North Richland Hills, there was an old, kind of dilapidated shopping center. One of its businesses was a dirty pawnshop in the corner. Not too appealing. Some of the other spaces were empty. The whole place was not too impressive…until you walked in the door of the space we were interested in renting. It was 9,000 square feet of genuine church. Formerly occupied by Believers' Fellowship and prior to that Living Word Fellowship (whose name was barely hanging on the marquee out front), the building was equipped with an auditorium complete with stage, sound booth, chairs and huge educational space with a large area for children and three small rooms for offices. It looked just right. Well, that would be after we took down some gaudy fixtures on the walls and some silver glittery fabric hanging from the ceiling over the auditorium stage. We had to make it our own, after all. We did. (Some churches like elaborate, showy stuff to worship the Lord. We like plain stuff.) And we rejoiced that we would not have to set up and tear down anymore! Most of us rejoiced, that is. Some of our group bemoaned the fact that there would be no more setting up and tearing down. It was then we learned the blessing of setup and tear down. Anyone can do it. You can be a part of a church and feel very significant without having to know the Bible very well, or how to pray in public. If you can unload a trailer and set up equipment, from baby cribs, to microphones and lights you are important…and definitely appreciated. Some of our new members were now not needed as much as before. Sad but true.

Four years we stayed in that shopping center. I have often wondered if I had been a Bear Valley mailer recipient would I have ventured to attend a "store-front church?" I knew I probably wouldn't have gone to a church meeting in a movie theater. What about a shopping center? I mean, is that "Church?" Fortunately, God's ways are not mine and fortunately God likes to do things outside of my particular box. We grew to an average attendance of about 250 at that location.

During those four Davis Blvd. years many people came to know Christ. We also attracted some adventuresome longtime Christians. I think of Jim and Wanda Gebhart. Wanda has been our church secretary for a long time now. Also there are Keith and Stacey Cartlidge, Peter and Kathy Kwaak, Dan and Karen Peterson, Lorrie and Greg Cheney and many others. Some lifelong friendships were made. Indeed "friendship" sounds too shallow a term. I would say some family ties were definitely made on Davis.

Having our own facility meant that we could have big meetings there any time we wanted. Becky Klute became known as the banquet lady, for the elaborate feasts she put on in the auditorium. Keith and Susan (Prather) planned some outstanding coffee houses, with not only great coffee, but also great talent being displayed for sometimes the first time in public. Even children's musicals were performed on the stage on Davis Boulevard. God brought the creatively musical Beth Lahaie to Bear Valley, and she got the children to performing. One summer she held a music camp in our facilities, teaching the children ALL aspects of music. One Christmas she directed a darling children's Christmas play that had all the children as different Christmas ornaments—coming out of a Christmas factory! I remember it well because I had a major part, as a grandmother-figure to all the children (with my white-sprayed hair). The night of the performance, the audience was packed with friends and family. What fun! Laura was a bell, I think, and Will was a nutcracker. Beth eventually became our children's director, as she was a natural for the job.

What made us even think about moving from that Davis shopping center was the problem with parking. Inside we had plenty of room, outside not nearly enough. Before we moved, though, Sam thought it might be good if we went to two services. As with any change in a church, there is criticism in the flock. If we had two services, then we couldn't all be together at the same time. We'd lose our sense of community. We'd all have to work harder, and longer. It just wouldn't be as much fun. Yada yada yada. And the more complaints I heard, the more I had to placate. That's the way it is with people pleasers. But there was no way I could placate everyone. I could try to talk Sam out of this bad decision, but I would just smile and tell the complaining church members, "Talk to Sam." One quality that has served Sam well in leading a church is stubbornness. When he sees what needs to be done, no amount of convincing, or manipulation—especially that—from anybody (especially his wife) will change his mind. And fortunately that trait kept us from plateauing as a church. Two services were announced, advertised and actualized...and we started seeing new people coming to Christ. It was exciting.

Here's an age-old question: when should you add a second service? I heard Rick Warren say that whenever you can average 70 people in the new service, you should add it. We call this critical mass. The more accurate principle is based upon the room size. The room cannot feel empty. A room that holds 200 people will feel full at 70. A room of 500 won't. Sometimes you can adjust the room size by using partitions (or pipe and drapes). Here's the exception to the second service: A friend of mine, Doug Walker, pioneered the concept of a worker service. He added a non-publicized early service at the very start of moving into a storefront. It was for workers in the children area only. When the church grew, needing a second service, then he would begin to advertise it. This solved most of the problem of burning out the workers in the children area and prepared the church for the addition of the second service. Btw, if you can start a church at 300, most of the growing issues are already behind you. That means you need to have 500 in your first service... When you know how to consistently do this, please write a book for the rest of us. Here are the only ways I have heard of: 1) Have a huge donor base to pay for a team (plus do everything else right). 2) Somehow assemble a large core group; like maybe, a church split or a giant youth group. One could assemble a large core through a series of house churches, but these networks tend to remain as a network of house churches. I do believe that the emerging multi-site movement has a good chance of consistently breaking the 300 barrier at start-up. (see <u>Multi-Site Road Trip</u>; although call me about how to organize *one of these. It's complicated. I got to do this after leaving Bear Valley.)*

To keep up with the growth, more workers had to be enlisted. When few came forward yours truly filled in. After the song service in the main auditorium I would run to the children's department and teach a Sunday School lesson. I really enjoyed that, but it required a good rest every Sunday afternoon. Preaching two services was quite exhausting for Sam, of course, also. Both of us were glad we didn't have Sunday night services at Bear Valley. Sam has noted through the years that planning and executing the Sunday morning service(s) at Bear Valley would take more time than doing the three unique services in a traditional church (Sunday morning and night, and Wednesday night). We did have lots of small groups meeting throughout each week, but Sam was not responsible for them. Once every two or three months, we'd have our classes 101, 201, 301, 401 on Sunday evenings, but that was all.

It's very important to keep your church simple and focused on activities that cause growth. We focused on three: 1) Sunday morning, 2) small group Bible studies and 3) targeted training for existing leaders. The many events Nancy mentions were permitted because members wanted to do these understanding that church resources would not be used. For example, the children's musical was done without the help of a staff member or budget. At the same time, these events allowed us to identify leaders who could then be strategically recruited for the focused events. As I read this section, I wish I had been more careful to include my wife's time as part of the church's resources. It just about finished her off before we got a han-

dle on it. I remember reading years ago that the one profession where the wife's expectancy is shorter than her husband, is in the ministry.

On Davis we had someone to teach most of the regular classes. Originally I taught 201, about growing spiritually. While we were on Davis I was promoted to teaching 401, on how to share your faith (odd, that—since I have had such a struggle with witnessing in my life). Fortunately, we had some good Willow Creek Church material, and it was nonthreatening to everyone, including its teacher. Sam taught 101, which was a course telling about our church, and about the Gospel and what Christianity is. Most people who become members at Bear Valley do so in that class. This is also where most people make a personal commitment to Christ. In the early days about 2/3's of the attenders of 101 were soon baptized as new followers of Christ. All of these classes were largely modeled after the Rick Warren baseball diamond.

Greg Goins, a hefty-looking weight-lifter and a student at Criswell Bible College in Dallas, taught my old class, 201. Tim Bobo, our associate pastor, taught 301, which was a great class designed to identify spiritual gifts and talents in its class members. I, then, taught 401. The classes would last four hours from four to eight, with a supper break at 5:45. For a while different small groups would bring the supper. Sometimes it would be sandwich fixin's, other times, pizza, or lasagna, or even spaghetti. When we'd worn out the small groups, we'd just order Dominos. I still have their number memorized. If this is making you hungry, dial 817-355-8888. Never did we have as good meals as we had at the home of Judie and Jimmy

Miller, though. By the time we'd moved to Davis, they had moved as well, to Burleson, TX.

In the shopping center on Davis, I found myself reverting back into trying to please every bloke in every way. Where was my lesson on God loving me regardless? When I look back and think of all I got involved in, I marvel that I didn't crater. Well, I almost did, until I sought out Dr. Barris Ayres as a counselor. I had been having insomnia again and Sam recommended I see Barris for a few weeks. Maybe Barris could help me get a grip—so I could sleep at night. My, did he. I am one of his cheerleaders now. I'll tell anyone who will listen that he is the best.

When we started Bear Valley, Sam knew that he needed to find a good Christian counselor to whom he could refer members. As you may know many pastors find themselves counseling church members. But most pastors, including Sam, are NOT professional counselors. A good pastor knows that often people with problems need a person who is trained to help them.

My rule-of-thumb: anyone who needs more than three sessions needs something better than me (sic). I can give Biblical advice. A good counselor is trained to give therapy (as well as Biblical advice). Also, a pastor who counsels often hurts the growth of his church. After sharing deep personal information a member usually is not comfortable listening to sermons from their counselor, so they leave.

This makes me think of how I've changed from being a dogmatic, judgmental holy joe, to an all-truth-is-God's-truth grace-filled believer (which is how I'd like to think of myself).

Back in the 1980's I read books by Dave Hunt (<u>Seduction of Christianity</u> and <u>Beyond Seduction of Christianity</u>) and became convinced that anything related to psychology or therapy or counseling was man's attempt to do what only God could do: heal the mind and soul. Even attempts to improve one's self-image was viewed as "not-of-God." (I'm serious.) I don't know exactly how I came across Hunt's books but in my zeal for following God I devoured anything that I thought would help me in my growth towards Him. I should have put a "WHOA" sign on Dave Hunt, because it took me years to unlearn what he tried to teach me in his books.

The desire for good self-esteem, according to Hunt, is of this world, certainly not of God. And any and all "Christian counseling" should be approached with caution if approached at all, particularly if the counseling is to promote self-esteem. The Bible is all one needs for a stable mind, and besides that one shouldn't esteem self at all. Self is to be denied, period. Luke 9:23 is his rallying cry.

That sounds really good, Mr. Hunt, but what about the whole Bible? It teaches us all about love. God's love for us, our love for him, and for others AS WE LOVE OURSELVES.

I can't remember what exactly was the tipping point on my turning from the Dave Hunt view to what I call my enlightened-by-grace view, but I am so glad I came to my senses—and became in favor of HOWEVER God can help me through life.

Fortunately, by the time my twin sister died and I was having major grief issues that I thought were spiritual problems (I should be happy Peggy's in heaven, right? What is the matter with me?), did I come to see that yes, there ARE good Christian counselors out there who can help. They're not all of the devil. HA! (Sometimes you (I) just have to relearn things.) (How I relearned that was to see how much a Christian counselor in Lawton helped some church members in Chattanooga. It was amazing...and I credit Sam for being wise to hunt out this counselor so she could help them.) I ended up going to her in 1989... and she helped me, by giving me permission to grieve Peggy's death, and to give me tools to get back to a productive life.

Well, I digressed some. (I just wanted to show how far I've come.)

Back to finding Barris: There was a man, a member of Northwood (whose name we cannot remember) who wanted to help get Bear Valley started, but whose wife, for some reason, was really hesitant to come on board. He really, really wanted to help us in spite of that, so we agreed to meet with him at a Pizza Hut in Keller.

I remember having an overwhelming feeling that I should meet with this person, that somehow he was important for Bear Valley.

"This is a waste of time," I thought, but Sam had a unique sense that this person was of vital importance to our church, which as it turned, in an indirect way, he was. I'm glad God doesn't let me run things. If I had been in charge we would have never heard about Barris... Because in the course of the conversation of how this man wanted to help us but couldn't, Sam asked him if he knew of a good counselor in the area to whom Sam could refer people. Without hesitation he said Barris Ayres. He is young, but he is wise beyond his years. So the Pizza Hut evening brought forth much fruit!

At the end of our meeting I was wondering if I had been mistaken about the importance of this meeting; then the thought occurred, maybe this is a meeting to obtain a referral to a key person and asked about a good counselor in the area.

So when Sam's wife began needing help, Sam referred her (me) to Barris.

I don't know what goes on in counselors' minds (probably a lot of eye-rolling) but I'm thinking Barris must have thought right away: Here's another "basket-case." I so appreciate that he let me just cry and cry…and get it all out. (As I look back, those tears were really from exhaustion, not major grief or anything.)

When I scheduled that first appointment, I knew I was getting burned out on everything. With his help, I realized that my problem was not so much going to be solved by getting out of stuff, but by realizing what made me get into stuff in the first place. I had thought my problem was everybody wanting a piece of me. My problem was in me letting them have one or two. For one thing I was too busy. I had kept leading Bear Club on Tuesday nights. It was getting bigger and bigger and that means more work, and more workers needed to help. I hate asking for help from anybody, so I got by with running myself ragged. I would lead the sing-a-long time, game time, Bible story time, and even bring the refreshments and lead that time.

If I had a helper they would just be there to make sure no one ran out into the street.

I also began a Wednesday night ladies' Bible study group. This was great, until we got a very needy lady to come and she dominated our time with her woe-telling. This sounds so crass. If I were leading that group nowadays, I would have handled it so much differently and not allowed the whole group time to be her therapy session. (In everything I do, I learn what not to do. When I'm old and decrepit I guess I won't do anything. Hmm. Life will be easy then.) I digress. Besides leading that night group I started a day group. This group was started because of my inability to say no. I had really thought my plate was full, but I guess I decided I would just get a bigger plate when I was approached by some young mothers and asked to lead their day group. Childcare was going to be a problem and a baby-sitter was hired by one of the group members. One of my pet peeves in life is unreliable people. That baby-sitter proved to be one of them. It was decided that we would just meet in the children's area and let the little ones play among us while we studied the Bible together. Bad idea. (Another thing I won't do again.) I had thought that since we were all mothers, we wouldn't mind the noise and distraction of little ones. Wrong. I found myself dreading those meetings, because of the chaos...and I didn't blame the children. Have you ever been with parents who let their kids get away with stuff? You find yourself wanting to start mothering their young yourself. Enough said.

The book I chose for that Bible study was absolutely wonderful. It met all my needs so, of course, it would meet theirs. It was <u>How To Leave Yourself Alone</u> by

Eugenia Price. I would spend hours getting ready for the group meeting and then afterwards would go home thinking I had done a wowy job (in spite of all the little rascals running around screaming and their mothers letting them). Pride does go before the fall. One day, one of those young women asked me out to lunch. At lunch, she began telling me how that the book I had chosen was just not where those women were at, and that they weren't getting anything out of my study. It was hard to tell me this, she said. She had no idea how hard it was for me to hear it. All that work, (I had made elaborate handouts each week, besides my own detailed notes) and it was not appreciated, not one iota. What was I to do? I sat there stunned. After a moment I began apologizing profusely for not meeting their needs and for not realizing it. One thing I have perfected in life is The Apology. As I look back on it with a much clearer mind, I see the fault of hers, in not letting me know sooner how I had "failed" these women. Hello!?! We've been studying that book for weeks and weeks. I was in my element. Well, I guess I was the only one in it. At this juncture you would think I would have resigned and let someone else take the group-lead. I tried…weakly. They wanted me as their leader, for some reason, but they just wanted me to pick a different topic and book, and do that. Should I have said, "No thank you?" Yes, I should have, but did I? Incredibly no. As I write this—my record of Bear Valley's history—I see what an education I have received through it all. And it mainly comes down to how I have learned NOT to do things. How to Just Say No. Well, in short, I did lead that group for a few more weeks on different topics they wanted to discuss, and then I bowed out. The group ultimately dissolved, but I don't blame myself. I tried.

I also started a monthly ladies large group meeting that I called LIFT (Ladies in Fellowship Together). In our Kentucky church we had a LIFT every month, and it was fantastic. Surely this would be. NOT. I did it for a whole school year and only about eleven women came in all. I so enjoyed planning the meetings. We'd talk about simplifying your life, where we'd trade easy recipes, and hints on how to clean a toilet really fast, etc. Then we'd have a devotional thought that I would bring, about simply trusting Jesus. That kind of thing. I loved it and thought it was great. Why didn't more women show up? The ones who did come loved it as well. Too bad most of our women were working moms and they just didn't have the time for another night out during the week. That reason makes more sense than they didn't like me, surely.

Every October when we were at the shopping center, I'd round up whichever ladies wanted to go and we'd make a trip to Canton Trades Day. What a hoot. We'd have a good group for that, and it was easy to do. Just show up and go. If Penny Holmes is reading this, she'll remember my expression as I thought I heard a flat tire going out on the van we borrowed from Northwood. Sure enough… Fortunately, God provided a highway patrolman to fix that tire. That was a fun day.

One February Saturday, I had a Ladies' Day which was a super hit with the women. We (I) called it "How to Be Beautiful—Inside and Out." The morning was spent dealing with inner beauty. I had a friend come and share how to have a quiet time with God. Then we had a salad lunch, from salads and desserts I had bought at Sam's Club. (It would be a few years before I learned how to ask people to help me—I'm not a quick study.) In the afternoon we had makeovers! Mary Springer taught us how to put on makeup and gave out lots of samples from Estee Lauder. Then Cindy Burnham taught us tricks on how to do our hair so it would flatter our face. When we went home that afternoon, we all looked and felt much prettier. As I recall, though, the next day we were back to our normal looks. A few of us spiffed up, but I don't know if anybody could tell. Ah, but we had fun.

I look back and see how much energy I spent on the women of Bear Valley. It was amazing. I also led yearly one-night women's retreats at Riverbend, near Glen Rose. They were fun and very popular. Later we'd do more elaborate retreats in places like Galveston, Mo Ranch in the Texas Hill Country, San Antonio and in East Texas for the weekend of Canton Trades Day. Each one of these was fantastic, if I do say so, but involved increasingly more work as the groups got larger, and the retreats got longer. One two-day retreat (Galveston) we invited the ladies to come early if they wanted to and have three days away from their housework and kids. Another lesson for me: Don't invite women to do things unless you're happy to take care of keeping up with their extra expenses, and also hearing their sometimes silly complaints. I told someone that I would love leading women's retreats if it weren't for the women!

Yes, I have also said that I would love ministry if it weren't for the people. That does sound cynical and sarcastic. I'm guilty of both. Seriously, though, ministry can be wonderful and yet it can be very hard. That's the way of any and all relationships, I guess. And as negative as I get about it all, I would not want to NOT be in ministry. It's where the love is. And I pray that Jesus would flow through me in spite of myself.

So Barris helped me. IMMENSELY. Later he joined our church...and eventually became our worship leader! The telling of that will be later.

I'm glad Nancy gave you a selected list of her many activities. We developed some strategies to avoid having our life dissolve into the fabric of the church. This included breaks both weekly and yearly, but more importantly becoming experts at healthy relationships...real community.

Most organizations tend toward dysfunction: manipulation, triangles, politics, etc.; all of them can devour your joy and undercut your effectiveness. Become an expert on setting healthy boundaries and never responding to unhealthy motivations pushed toward you by others: guilt, shame, approval, to name a few. Nancy and I learned to ask each other, are we letting someone else be God to us? Who are we trying to please? Are we doing this to please God or please someone else?

If you especially struggle with healthy boundaries buy the book <u>Boundaries</u>, by Townsend and Cloud. If you don't, buy it anyway. It really is one of the better books written. Then as you learn to understand better, here's a strategy you might try: Use the acrostic D.I.D.—Detach, Identify and Decide. As you find yourself living from the expectations of others, you'll begin to recognize it, stopping yourself before you say "Yes" (detach). Think through what you are about to do and devise a better plan (iden-

tify). You are about to let someone's opinion count more than your own. Worse yet...more than God's. Decide to do what creates real community.

My fears have basically revolved around acceptance, approval, people-pleasing—and all the "shoulds" and "oughts" that come with that. If I sense someone has expectations of me, I try to meet those expectations perfectly...or I try and bolt fast. I'm doing the latter more lately.

Here are some things Sam did to help me:

Sam helped me by telling me I had a veto-right, a right to nix what he wanted to do if I just didn't feel I could do it.

Sam started referring to our new church start as a "piano bar" sensitive to Christians, as opposed to sensitive to seekers. That gave me a super sense that I was integrally a part of this endeavor (since I was the piano player).

Sam always asked me about inviting people over. He didn't just invite folks over and blindside me with it. I'm pretty private. Sadly, on occasion, I haven't given him the same courtesy, though I'm trying to be better.

Sam has always told me I didn't have to be a part of anything...or do anything. I was always the one trying to start a new group, etc., because I thought I "should."

Sam has always given me grace to be who I am.

On Davis, Sam and I grew in many ways. The shopping center days were rich. We would have stayed there much longer if it weren't for the parking. Even at two services we found ourselves running out of space, primarily parking. On Easter, and other big days, we would have our members park across busy Davis Blvd. at the Liberty Bank parking lot.

What brought a lot of people to our church were our fun Halloween Magic Shows. We had started those in the movie theater and made them an annual tradition. In the shopping center, lots of extra chairs would have to be set up to accommodate the crowds. Both Sam and Tim Bobo were (are) professional magicians, so it made for a very entertaining, professional show. That we held them on Sunday mornings, made them very interesting indeed. We'd send out carefully crafted mailers inviting one and all to come and see Carmack the Incredulous and Bobo, the "Bonderful" (I made that last one up). Two different times in two different mailers we made some big blunders. In one we advertised what was supposed to be a "mock séance." Of course, it would be mock, since we are a Christian church and the purpose of our magic show is not just entertainment but to share the love of Jesus, albeit in an entertaining manner. The mailer was somehow not proofread well enough. It went out without the word "mock." Now that would not seem like such a problem, but to our anti-Halloween Christian friends it was a major problem. How could we be called a church and be having a séance? A magic show was bad enough, a séance was completely of the devil. It is amazing how unchristian Christians can sound when they are making anonymous phone calls about something they think is unChristian. It should be said here that we used to design our advertising to actually discourage Christians from attending our services. We wanted our church to be made of new Christians and those considering Christianity. This is called a Conversion Growth Church as compared to a Transfer Growth Church. Hopefully either type will be Missional.

Speaking of phone calls, our next magic show mailer blunder involved the wrong phone number printed. That would not sound so bad if no one else had that wrong number. When spotting the wrong number, Sam immediately called it and apologized to the man at that number. The man said he did not see any problem and was quite supportive. That attitude changed in a few days, understandably. He called us irate, telling us that "everyone" is calling and complaining and they wouldn't believe it was a wrong number. We, of course, became determined to carefully proofread every future Halloween mailer, taking special care to see the phone number was correct. We also eventually adopted the saying, "if no one calls complaining about the mailer, then we have failed in reaching our target audience."

The magic shows came about largely by accident. By the time the first Halloween came around, I was so tired of producing quality services, that I thought I would pull an old act out of the bag, having worked as a magician when in college. Wow, what a surprise. It actually became one of our best growth days. We would tie a portion of the service to the upcoming series and had a fairly high rate of return visitors. It also served a second purpose. Some people felt churches like ours were too entertaining, at the expense of preaching the gospel. I would start this service out mentioning this fact and point out: we do this service to show you what entertainment truly is. Of course, we would find clever ways to teach scripture throughout the service.

Peter Kwaak likes to remind me that it was a Halloween service when he first came: little church background, just curious, and became one of the key leaders in our international ministry, small group pastor and church trustee. Gathering people for an event is only a single step in the conversion process, which transforms lives and communities.

Pertaining to entertainment, I remember one lady who shared with me after a service that she was going to return to the church of her youth, having been reached for Christ by our church. When I asked why, she said, with tears in her eyes, "I enjoy your church so much that I feel guilty." This is a good setup for James Brown.

chapter 7

James Brown

> "I have become all things to all men so that by all possible means I might save some. I do all this for the sake of the gospel..." (1 Cor. 9:22-23 NIV)

Perhaps the most interesting story about our four years on Davis Boulevard has to do with Gary and Debbie Long. One day Debbie was driving down Davis, wondering if maybe it was time for her and Gary to start going to church again. About that time she drove by the shopping center and saw our church sign. Just then she heard her favorite song on the radio, "I Feel Good," by James Brown. A few days later she was driving by again, and again "I Feel Good" came on the radio. Hmm, she thought. Maybe that is some kind of sign. The next Sunday she and Gary walked in our door, and our opening music started. Keith Prather and the band were doing "I Feel Good." This story sounds like fiction. It is not. From that day on, Gary and Debbie became active members of our church and Gary, a former owner of the roadie company that worked with Aerosmith and Eric Clapton (yes, you read that right), made our eventual move to the schools as effortless as possible. He made big boxes for our equipment, and ran our set-up and tear-down with skill and expertise that could not be matched by anyone. He also plays a mean harmonica and accompanied our band on many occasions. "I Feel Good" has been a special song for Bear Valley since then. No one can hear that tune without thinking of that incredible story.

This makes me want to stop and just talk for a bit about Bear Valley's music. It was decided early on that, if possible, we needed to do songs people knew. I mentioned earlier that some folks didn't know "Amazing Grace." Well, what songs did the people we were trying to reach know? Clearly "I Feel Good" was one of them. But there were lots. Doing them well was the challenge. Having band members who were in the prestigious University of North Texas music school was the answer to that challenge. They made it possible for us to "cover" lots of tunes. We've done everything from James Taylor to Tom Petty and the Heartbreakers. A particularly good song we did was when Amy Bobo sang "One of Us" by Joan Osborne. You'd have thought Joan was right there, if you hadn't seen Amy on the stage. We nailed STYX "Show Me the Way," which even if you'd never heard it, you'd resonate with it the first time. We did Doobie Brothers' music, Celine Dion's... Of course we also covered Christian artists, like Margaret Becker, Susan Ashton and Amy Grant.

The reason I know all of these is because I spent many an hour working on backups and/or keyboard charts for these songs. There was awhile I just got too stressed playing keyboard for these songs, because to make them sound like they do on the CDs, well, it was pretty daunting for this amateur to pull off. We did get help, though. Amy played for a while, and then we got some professional players from University of North Texas. One was named Daniel and he was from Sweden! Ah, but we only got him because he knew Niclas and Sara Hoglind, our Swedish player and singer with the mostest!!

Nic and Sara could make up a whole chapter in this book, if not a whole book by itself. Nic began playing lead guitar for us in the Davis location. He was incredible. And then we found out his wife Sara had one of the most amazing voices in the universe. Unfortunately they moved back to Sweden, but before they did, their first-born child, a beautiful daughter, Hildur, was born. Since she's an American and particularly a TEXAN!, well, they have special ties here. (And I must tell you that when Sam and I visited our daughter who was studying abroad in Florence, Italy in 2006, well, we took the excuse of being nearby (kind of!) and visited them in Sweden.)

Back to the music: we covered lots of tunes in the Bear Valley band. I think we used Eagles' tunes more than any, and their "New York Minute" was the song that we will NEVER forget.

I'm going to copy and paste here what Barris Ayres wrote as a comment to my blog post commemorating the tenth anniversary of the World Trade Center bombing of 9/11. Barris wrote:

> I rarely post comments, but this one really commands my attention. I was Music Pastor at our church at the time. It really was one of the strangest moments of my life.
>
> That morning I was hard at work learning a featured song we were going to be presenting the following Sunday. I think the song was il-

lustrating a point in the message's topic of "time management" or something like that.

I had been up early and was taking a break to check email, etc. when I read the story on the internet. One tower had just been hit and no one knew quite what was going on.

My first reaction was, "This can't be real...this is some kind of gag...some kind of publicity stunt..." but then I watched as the second plane hit the other tower, and the horror of the insidious nature of this being planned was undeniable. Then it got worse as I saw the towers collapse knowing all the rescue people who died in that instant, having knowingly and unselfishly run into harm's way.

Some break, huh? Feeling helpless I thought I should at least get back to learning my song, and wondered if this crisis would change our plans for the service. Then I realized the song we had already planned to do was perfect for this unexpected situation..."New York Minute" by Don Henley.

Originally we had planned to do the song for another reason, but as the meaning of the lyrics washed over me, I realized that perhaps God had allowed us to be prepared in advance for all the people in our church who would be in shock and mourning. "In a New York Minute, everything can change...in a New York minute things can get pretty strange...and in these days when darkness falls early and people rush home to the ones they love... You'd better take a fool's advice and take care of your own, cause one day they're here, the next day they're gone."

> In that instant I absolutely knew that God was going to use our church to help heal somehow, and even amidst all the sorrow I had such a real conviction that God's hand was on us to help us through this time…

In that service we added graphics of the towers and their destruction. I'm sure we all remember the American flag picture from that day. Btw, I think the service topic was Priorities.

Using "secular" music was what we needed to do at Bear Valley. And it could be very powerful, particularly on that Sunday after 9/11.

Pop music (and movies) are the primary expression of values in our culture today. Especially for children of the 60's and 70's. Often we can find common values or common struggles in pop music which make it easier to start the conversations with the skeptic or spiritually curious.

The use of pop music helps prevent the division between Sunday and weekdays—the secular and sacred. We discovered that as we infused Christian meaning into pop songs, it helped our members to experience that the whole week belongs to the Lord.

It helps the skeptic to feel welcomed and affirmed when the church says, "We like your music and we find meaning in it."

Using pop music worked well for baby boomers. We all listened to the same music and much of the music was very much about values. Sometimes a fellow pastor would object to our use of pop music and I would simply ask, "Do you sometimes quote lyrics of a pop song as an illustration in your sermon?" Of course he did. "Why not quote it along with music... Sing it."

A huge amount of resources were poured into the Sunday morning hour, but we knew the real secret to spiritual growth resided in the small group structure. From the very start small groups provided the foundation for Bear Valley. We wanted to be a church of small groups and not a church with small groups. To do this we treated every people-process as a small group process. For example, the music team was first of all a real community built around small group dynamics. The Trustees began every meeting with a small group Bible discussion and prayer. I would have the staff to my house regularly where we focused mainly on group prayer and Bible discussion. We taught that the first line of care came from the small group structure. If someone goes to the hospital, it is the small group that administers care. We used Rick Warren's line: You don't want to be so sick that the senior pastor would need to visit you.

Here's what is interesting: A church below the 200 barrier (average attendance) really can get by pretty well without small groups. The community time needed for happy church members can happen on Sunday morning, especially true when below 100 which is the average family reunion size. This experience of community is no longer possible once the church moves past the 200 to 300 hundred barrier. At this point, some type of sub-grouping has to happen in order to experience real community, which is vital for spiritual growth.

Here's the really important principle: From the very start, organize your church for 1,000 and not just for 100.

We built the small group structure into the church from the very start, so when we grew beyond 200, we already had the infrastructure in place. At the time we started we used the book, <u>Prepare Your Church for the Future</u>, by Carl George. The best book I know of now is <u>Activate</u>, by Nelson Searcy. In fact, all of Nelson Searcy's books are great.

Here's an important truth: Significance comes from the big Sunday event; true joy comes from real community in a small group of believers. You need both.

chapter 8

New Vision

> "If people can't see what God is doing, they stumble all over themselves; But when they attend to what he reveals, they are most blessed."
> (Proverbs 29:18 Message)

Our time on Davis was very fruitful. Many people came to Christ while we were there. We were seeing, though, that unchurched people who come to the Lord, for the most part take a while before they see the need to tithe or even give any of their resources to the church. I was even asked one day what the word "tithing" meant. I was reminded of how I had been immersed in christianese and didn't realize it when the young man pronounced "tithing" with a short i.

Because we were reaching so many people for the Lord who did not yet give to Him and His church, we were pretty strapped financially. That meant, for one thing, no money for a janitor. It was a great idea Sam had to form a small group just for the purpose of cleaning the facility on Saturdays to get ready for Sundays. Some people volunteered to be in that group and enjoyed coming, having a short Bible study and prayer time and then getting to work. Going "two by two" to clean—it is amazing how many Bible verses there are that can be applied to cleaning. On some occasions, of course, they all couldn't show up. Sam, I and Will and Laura took up that slack. I can recall many times when we'd be there cleaning restrooms, vacuuming, etc., on Saturday afternoons. It made me appreciate all the janitors I have met through the years.

The four years on Davis were fun. Well, sometimes not, but most times yes. Even with two services, though, we were running out of parking space. What to do? Move? That seemed our only option, since we did not have the personnel, nor the inclination to go to more services. Sam began looking at moving the church to a school. That would mean set-up and tear-down each week, but we knew there were some advantages to that. He began asking around and found that the Grapevine Colleyville School District would let churches meet in their facilities, but only if the church owned property in Colleyville or Grapevine and had the intention to build within two years. Sam was eager to buy property and knew he could get a good loan to do it. Where, though? I have always known Sam to be a good decision maker, and deliberating for as long as it takes to make a good decision. In this one, he did just that. I had thought north Precinct Line Road was too far out there. I was so wrong. We bought the land when the road was just two lanes full of potholes, knowing that someday it would widen. That someday came really soon. (That $380,000 piece of property is now valued at about $2 million.)

I must say that at this point in the life of the church, I found myself in a bit of a crisis. My goals as a church *planter had been rather modest. I believed that if after ten years I had grown a church which ran 200, and half of those attending came from the unchurched community, conversion growth, then it would have been well worth the effort. I found myself at this point with the vision for a church of two hundred running 250. I didn't have a vision beyond that. I took off a few days for prayer and spent time visiting with a close friend, Dr. Lee Johnson. I don't remember how it came about, but I returned with a new vision. A new confidence that we were to become a church which ran six hundred, with property and multiple buildings. The plan was to pick a good piece of land, which would escalate in value. Pay for the land. Do a second fundraiser for the building, which would then allow us to build; using the land, a second fund raiser and new building as collateral to finance the building. Obtaining a hard asset, property, and developing a budget ready for a loan payment was key at this stage of growth. It took about three years, but it worked well. When I left the church it had surpassed 650 and had ten acres of land with a master plan for a church of 3,000. We also had designed the second building and raised $900,000 in pledges. The second building cost 1.6 million dollars.*

Now that we had land we could rent the cafetorium (combination cafeteria and auditorium) of an elementary school. A high school or middle school was really what we wanted, but they (school district) would only permit use of an elementary school. We started using Bransford School on Glade, just a block off of Highway 26 (for $250 an hour).

It is amazing to me that people would get a mailer and actually checkout a church meeting in a school. I have to say that I don't think I would. I guess I just don't think outside of the box enough. But that's the kind of people we've attracted. Those who think outside the box. What a great kind of folk that is!

Before they could come to the services at the school though, we'd have to set up. We'd get there around 7:30 each Sunday morning. Before that, though, we'd have to get the donuts, and then the trailer. We (Sam, Will, Laura and I), would go to the donut shop at Harwood and Highway 121 to pick up the donuts. Not to miss an opportunity to make a family tradition, we began arriving at the Sunshine Donut Shop early to have our fun breakfast (we did this every Sunday morning before we'd set up at the movie theater also). Picking out a donut from a bevy of beauties is a challenge. I usually stuck with the glazed cake kind, Sam would get a bear claw or a twister, and Will and Laura would get something different each week. Then we'd sit at a little table and enjoy. Often Laura would sit on her daddy's lap because she was cold. (It actually gets cold sometimes in Texas.)

Hmm. I'm thinking Will, Laura, Sam and I need to do a "do-over" at that donut shop one of these mornings. (Yeah, it might be fun to have Will and Laura and their spouses help them—and us—take a trip down memory lane someday. I know that I would enjoy it.)

Then we'd arrive at the school. Again, I say, no one appreciates what goes on in setting up and tearing down a church who hasn't DONE IT!!

Ah, but we did it…for two more years…and we became quite proficient at it. Well, we really had a lot of help during this stage. Sam had a staff member in charge of the trailer and setup, Jeff Clack. We also had a youth director, children's director, music director, secretary and business administrator. This also was the period when we found Lee Johnson as we were getting ready for the new building. And we had about thirty small groups as well. Lee's story will be told a little later, but you can see we were ripe for his addition to the staff.

Meeting in the schools meant that we needed office space again. Near Harwood and Precinct Line in Hurst there came open a spot that fit us to a T. By then, we had a part-time administrator, one of my most favorite people in the world, our former youth director, Julie Zuefeldt. I want to stop here and tell you a little about Julie.

She had been on staff at our sponsor church, Northwood, and I'd heard her name often, always spoken with great praise. To think that she would come on board at Bear Valley was a dream come true. She first helped out in our youth program...and that's where I got to really start knowing her. She and I held a sleepover at Diane Bowden's house (thank you, Diane!) back in '93 for teenage girls. The evening was spent watching a video by Josh McDowell on "Why Wait" (till marriage for sex) and then we had hair and make-up tips given by Cindy Burnham. Back then most girls (and I) wanted to know how to have our bangs shoot up from our forehead just so. Cindy taught us that...and Julie and I giggled most of the time.

Julie and her family, (husband Dan, daughter Rebekkah and twins Stefan and Gretchen) became an integral part of Bear Valley. Now she is called Executive Pastor and has been known to speak at many of the services. She is a natural communicator.

Julie first helped us as a consultant, teaching some of our new Christians how to run a youth program. When she accepted a staff position, first as youth director, then as executive pastor, she completed a vital link in our management team. I was good at creating, visioning, teaching, etc. I could maintain existing programs, but not with joy. She enjoyed maintaining already existing programs and improving on what already had been created. Usually all of these qualities do not exist in the same person, creation vs. maintenance/development. It takes a team with the right people working in the right area.

Julie enjoys keeping things working well as they are. Change, however, was not as easy. Julie wrote:

> Bear Valley Church opened up my eyes to a whole new way of doing ministry. Being a part of this new way to reach people for Christ was life changing for me. I don't think I would have gone down this road if it weren't for Sam and Bear Valley. Sam had to keep reminding me who we were trying to reach and why we did the things we did. I would slowly go back to the way I was raised and Sam had to bring me back to this new way of ministry. Now I never want to go back to the old way again. God changed so many families through Bear Valley, it has been an honor and joy to be a part of it.
>
> —Julie Zuefeldt

Julie would be called, by management consultants, A Tool Box Person. When she views a situation / problem, she'll look into her toolbox and figure out which tool can fix it. To create a new tool would be much harder for her. Someone who would be called an Architect Person (that's

New Vision

me) is better at tool creation, but fairly quickly grows tired of the tool and wants to change it.

Here's another principle: If you start something rather unique, which might require a paradigm shift, realize that most people need to first experience it before they can understand it. A minority of the population has the brain wiring to visualize what you want to do before you do it. Here's the big challenge: those who are able to visualize it usually are not well suited to maintain it. It takes a team.

Around the time we made Julie Executive Pastor, we also hired a part-time youth director, seminary student Greg Ingram. Greg was (still is) a dynamic young man who would meet with our middle school and high schoolers every Sunday night in our living room. He also stayed in our house while we went on a trip one summer. The neighbors thought it was funny that he put up our Mary and Joseph Christmas light-statue in the yard in July. That was so his friends could find which house to come to for the party he was throwing (with our consent).

I've been trying to decide the best time to write about Rob. Along with Will and Laura, Sam and I, Rob has been with us since Bear Valley's beginning. He'd been in the background, because he was young. But he was growing up for sure…and the fact that he lived with Greg in our house that summer, well, that means now is the time I tell you about him.

Rob is our nephew, Sam's brother Steve's oldest son. When he turned sixteen we invited him to live with us for the summer, so he could work at Six Flags Over Texas, the dream job of every sixteen-year-old. Six Flags is about twenty minutes away from our house, so it seemed like a no-brainer.

He grew up in Hinton, Oklahoma, a wonderful town in western Oklahoma with a population of about 1,000. It's where Sam grew up, by the way, and it's where we lived when Will was born. There's one flashing red light at Main Street and Highway 281 and a few stop signs around town. That's where Rob got his driver's license. I guess I wasn't thinking the day he was to drive down to stay with us because it hadn't dawned on me what a major endeavor it would be for him to drive down to the Metroplex for the first time. When it was time for him to arrive and he didn't… I got concerned. Time passed, and we all got concerned. Finally he showed up. It's a small wonder that his dad trusted him to make that journey. Ah, but Steve trusted Rob to find his way—and did he!

So Rob lived with us, finding out after the first day at Six Flags, that it wasn't the wonder-job he thought it would be. But he persevered. He operated the Conquistador, which is known as the ride that makes people throw up. Oh, the stories he would tell, mainly of giving people free t-shirts when they got sick on that ride. We were proud that he lasted the whole summer.

The next summer, 1999, he lived with us as well, working at the nearby BlockBuster Video. His being a movie buff, that was right down his alley, and our being movie buffs, well, we liked to go see him work (which was sometimes just washing windows). It was during that time that he began feeling that maybe God was wanting him in the ministry, so he became Greg's assistant in the youth program.

Sometime in the early part of that summer Greg resigned as youth pastor. Since Rob had been working as his assistant, he stepped up to the plate and pretty soon he began rallying the youth together to go to church camp. He did a stellar job at that and so became our official youth director.

Everyone was so glad he chose to go to nearby Texas Christian University for college. That meant he could still be Bear Valley's youth director. (Most all of Rob's extended family have gone to Baylor in Waco.)

Rob did some awesome things with the youth. They went on mystery trips, and ski trips, and fun spring-break "overtimes." He got them to reading the Bible, and discovering for themselves God's truths. He would host meetings about doubt—and how doubt in God was okay, and could spur you on to faith. Always challenging them, Rob grew up a dynamic youth group who went on to change their world for the better. Two of those youth were my kids…so I am forever grateful.

Rob not only could lead a good youth program, but he could speak like no one else could (can). He started being on the speaking rotation at Bear Valley, and folks couldn't wait till it was his turn to speak, I being one of them. Soon he got on the speaking circuit around the state, speaking and leading youths at Discipleship Now weekends, and youth retreats, camps and rallies.

As I type this he is on staff at Fellowship of the Parks in Keller, Texas, as a teaching pastor, and as the senior pastor's main assistant. He also has a beautiful wife, Caroline, and two of the cutest little children you have ever seen, Sawyer and Delia.

There's more to tell about Rob, but that would take another book. I better get back to telling you about what I was talking about: the offices on Harwood and Precinct Line Road in Hurst.

About the time we hired Greg Ingram, we also hired a "techie" seminary student, Jeff Clack. Jeff was good at all things electronic, and he was also great in the area of drama and puppetry. His puppet skills were used on many occasions during the services. (Sometimes Kermit the Frog can get across a point so much better than a person can.)

Greg, Jeff, church secretary Wanda, Pastor Sam, administrator Julie, along with music director Keith, meant the rented office space was buzzing with activity daily.

The office facilities didn't take care of all the meetings, but that was okay for a while. Our music team started meeting in our home on Wednesday nights, as did our youth group on Sunday nights. I liked that a lot, for a while. Well, another lesson I learned was to not start something you don't want to keep going. Soda pop for instance. I started putting canned Cokes and Dr. Peppers on the bottom shelf of our fridge and everybody knew they could help themselves. Plus I made coffee and the same rule applied. Now that is a great thing to do—to offer refreshment to guests. You have to keep it up, though, and also you need to have something of a clean house when you have people over. Well, if you're like me and are worried about what people think of you, you have to. I was learning, though, again, that you don't HAVE to do anything. Unfortunately I'm not a quick study. It took me a while to learn that. So I kept the pop supplied, the coffee, and sugar, and creamer and sweet 'n low, and the cups and napkins, etc., replaced every week. I have since learned that when you have a group meeting in your home it is okay if they bring their own drinks. I was just glad I hadn't gotten cookies and cake started.

We also began hosting a small group of adults in our home on Thursday nights, and on occasion large groups of adults. I enjoyed these meetings, but they were all taking a toll on me. Many people are surprised to find out that I am basically an introvert. Though outgoing at times, I need privacy and alone time more than most people so I can recharge my batteries. Hosting weekly groups in my home, plus doing all the other church work I was doing, not to mention "mothering" and "wifing" was depleting my batteries big time. Somewhere along the road I quit taking care of myself. I'd forgotten what I learned from Barris, and well, just reverted back to burnout. In September of 1998 I developed a terrible case of hives from head to toe. I never completely discovered the cause, but I suspect it might have been stress. Now stress was a bad word for me. As a devoted follower of Christ I was not supposed to live my life in it. Of course, shaming myself for being stressed was causing stress.

Those hives turned out to be a good thing, though. In fact, they turned out to be just what I was needing to make me stop my madness of over activity. I started taking large doses of Benadryl to keep the hives at bay. Well, that knocked me out. I was good for nothing but lying around in a stupor. Then I dragged myself to the doctor's office where he gave me a big dose of the steroid Prednisone. That weekend Sam, Will and Laura and I were scheduled to go down to a Baylor football game. I just could not do it. I stayed home by myself for two days and during that time had my own personal revival. Of course, the steroid made me feel good and the Benadryl made me relaxed. Sometimes "feeling good" and "feeling relaxed" can be the same thing. I guess I was getting a double dose of relaxation…mmm… Whatever it was, I liked it, and understand how people can get addicted to pills. I had recently heard of the good of journaling and so I started writing and to this day I love reading those "memoirs" of my doped up, relaxed days back in '98. Journaling had never been such a catharsis before. It was like I was joyously vomiting up all the pent-up feelings I'd had about being a yes-person all my life, and I was giving myself permission to be a no-person for a change. It was glorious, and so needed. I had gotten (again) so, so busy doing church work that I had not realized how I neglected Nancy-work. Now I could do it—I had two days alone to get in touch with my inner self. Before I had berated people for navel-gazing too much. I'd had a certain disdain for pop psychology and I put deep introspection into that category, because it can be too selfish. Well, now I was letting myself be selfishly introspective, and I was so enjoying it. Admittedly, if I hadn't been drugged up on Prednisone and Benadryl, I would not have journaled with such abandon. I think I was needing the uninhibitedness that came with feeling euphoric and being completely alone for two days.

Those journal entries are therapy for me to this day. They give me permission to live within boundaries. I can say "No." I can live life on God's and my terms and not on everybody else's terms. I can quit letting my house be the church's fellowship hall. I can quit leading every Bible study group that wants a leader. I can quit, period. And I did! After that cathartic personal retreat God gave me, I told the music team to start looking for another place to meet. Janet McKinney started hosting it, and loved doing so. I still hosted Crossroads, the youth group meetings on Sunday nights, but I started putting up signs for the kids to clean up their messes before they left...and to empty their cups of liquid and ice before throwing them away. And I started insisting that everyone be out of the house by nine-thirty. Wow, it felt good to get control of myself and of our living space. And I let other adults be sponsors at preteen camp, and later youth camp. And I told Keith I needed to quit being responsible for getting all the music together for rehearsal and weekends. And at this stage of the church, there were plenty of people eager to assume meaningful responsibility.

I was on a roll. Life was good again. Oh every now and then I revert back to my old people-pleasing ways, trying to be everybody's everything, but then I remember Barris and my lessons with him, and that weekend in '98, and I am ready to face the world again. As I write this, I praise the Lord that He has taught me how to take care of myself...and that it is not selfish to do just that. It is wise.

Someone wiser than me once pointed out that the most valuable asset of the church is the senior pastor, and I would add, his wife. We are foolish when we fail to take care of these important assets of the church.

We spent two years setting up and tearing down in the elementary schools. When Bransford started remodeling, we moved to O. C. Taylor Elementary, which was nearer to our home. We had to meet a couple of weeks at Glenhope Elementary, but that was close to O. C. Taylor, so we just had a few men out front directing church goers to head that-a-way and it was fine. (We had been given just twenty-four hour notice that we'd have to move to Glenhope that first Sunday there.)

Meeting in a school had its advantages. We did not need to have janitorial services (our $250 an hour rent took care of that), and we didn't have to be out at 11:00 as we did in the movie theater. I'm trying to think of other advantages, but my head scratching is not working.

It's a place the whole community frequents and therefore it is neutral ground, not sacred territory.

As in all of our moves, some people came with us, some people did not. We'd usually shrink by about 10%, which is really not very much for a move. Some churches lose as many as 50%. Always, though, our moves meant we would reach new folks.

About this time Sam had one very important conversation with John Worcester (a church planting expert and close friend). Sam was considering dropping conversion-growth strategy during this period of being in the school and focusing upon discipleship of existing members during the main worship hour. John told him not to do that, that it would be very difficult to go back to conversion-growth church principles. Even if it is difficult to grow, be careful about changing the focus of the church.

We did make some changes…we quit using the word "seeker," and began emphasizing that Sunday morning was a worship period for believers, while including our whole community, not just church goers.

Throughout all the years, even to this day, Bear Valley has been reaching those people we call the "radically unchurched." They are the folks who are not steeped in "christianese" and who often have values that would be frowned upon if discovered in many a traditional church.

Like the lottery. We have had people who when they get their first Bible promptly go buy a lottery ticket so they can make it their Bible bookmark, hoping the Bible would be good luck in the next lottery drawing. We've also had a few people in small groups, who when prayer requests are asked for, ask for prayer that they would win the lottery so they could get out of debt. When we would ask for money, which we try not to do since it is a total turnoff for unchurched folk, someone will suggest that we play the lottery and pray for a big win, to help with our budget, or new building, etc.

Also, the topic of marriage will come up when a couple wants to join the church and find out that to be a member they need to either quit living together or get married. Usually these people know that what they are doing is unchristian. Sometimes not. When marriage is discussed it is often the desire of the woman to do it, and hesitance on the part of the man. Many a time, Sam has performed weddings for these couples that want to be members of our church. Only once that I can think of did he have a real (still awkward) problem getting the couple to make it legal. I am glad our church holds to the sanctity of marriage.

Some critics of our new-fangled kind of church accuse us of being liberal, in this regard and others. It is clear that these critics have not done their homework. Oh, we are definitely contemporary, but we are not liberal. We make it clear that we take the Bible literally and seriously.

I cherish a recent email from one of our mentored planters. You can do real worship / bible teaching and be seeker inclusive.

> As a Christian attending seminary, I was hungry for the Word of God. However, very few churches would teach the inspired, inerrant, and infallible Word of God from the pulpit. After receiving an invitation in the mail from Bear Valley, I found the sermon titles to contain strong biblical doctrine. I was frustrated after attending many churches that did not teach the Word of God, so I decided to try Bear Valley. This experience inspired me to start a church of my own. Yeshua Elohim Bible Church exists today because of the positive spiritual influence of Dr. Carmack and Bear Valley.
>
> —Dr. Bruce Foster

Take our position on homosexuality. Some times we would classify our sermons as R-rated and tell families that came that we would be treating an adult topic and that their children probably should not be in the service. Sam preached pointedly about what the Bible says about homosexuality; frankly, it was a little too graphic even for me.

I'm especially proud of the way we handled this topic at the time the Episcopal church appointed a gay bishop. Prior to the service Pastor Lee Johnson and youth director Rob Carmack (our nephew) interviewed the bishop of the Metropolitan Community Church. She let them videotape the interview and was very cordial throughout the session. While Rob was behind the video camera, Lee asked her questions such as, how do you deal with passages such as Leviticus 18:22 and Romans 1: 26, 27? Her answer was interesting. Wherever it was mentioned that homosexuality was a sin she would state that it is the view of her church that the passage meant heterosexuals doing acts that were not in their nature. It did not refer to homosexuals doing homosexual acts. That, she said, was fine. We need to "be who we are" and the Bible teaches to not be who we are not.

Our treatment of this issue of gayness was well thought out. As said before Bear Valley has been known through the years to be contemporary but not liberal. To approach a politically incorrect, conservative view in a polite manner has required much deliberation. As shown in the above story, the leaders of the church have not skirted issues, but have delicately presented the Biblical view of controversial ones. In the above case the bishop of the gay church was not lambasted for her beliefs. She was merely asked questions and allowed to answer them. After the videotape was shown the following weekend service, Lee merely read the scriptures again to let them speak for themselves.

One man, Andy Hollinger, was visiting for the first time that Sunday morning. He had been an atheist, a Marxist-Leninist, and a minister in the Universalistic/ Unitarian Church. A history professor in a local college, he was the definition of "erudite." To make a very long story short, our treatment of that "hot topic" was a factor in his giving Christianity a look, and his subsequent step of faith in Christ. In fact, during Andy's first meeting with Sam, Andy said (something to the effect) "You are the first fundamentalist preacher I've heard talking about gays that didn't make me mad."

Andy and I developed a great friendship and spent months meeting over coffee and email discussing faith related topics. I'll never forget the email that really mattered. Andy was in the midst of a long philosophical argument, when all of a sudden his sentence abruptly stopped. A couple of empty lines, then something along the line of, "Oh, heck! I'm just being proud... I'm in!" That may be one of the only email conversions of all history. It's been fun to see the change in Andy and his view of history, which is what he teaches. He's one of the better intellects I've known and count it a great honor to be present when God was doing his work within him.

So there was an example of treating a hot topic in a conservative, yet palatable manner. Though we've also addressed other topics that are rallying points with some churches, such as abortion, we really have not delved into some topics that others would (example: the lottery). I would say that we try to major on the majors and minor on the minors. I believe that comes from Rick Warren. Jesus Christ and his way of salvation is a major, major. To spend a lot of time on other topics is to divide instead of conquer.

I have digressed here so much that I must remind even myself of where I am in my story. Oh yes, setting up and tearing down in the elementary school. There is something humbling about meeting in a school. You don't have the beautiful building and the prestige that goes with the church building. I think there is something to be said for the way the church got started back in the first century. There were homes, and mountainsides, and maybe under shade trees. The Antioch church used a cave. How simple and unpretentious is that? Having started Bear Valley in an old, dirty movie theater, and then moving to a run-down looking shopping center with a dusty pawnshop next door, and now in an elementary school, my feelings for big nice buildings had almost turned to judgmentalism. I confess the I'm-better-than-you idea I have carried since starting this church. I tell others that I'm not against traditional churches, it's just that God has called us to start this new-fangled thing, and I must follow His lead. It is my way of being a missionary. That sounds kind of holier-than-thou. It's true. One of my struggles in all this has been that I HAVE been prejudiced against the traditional church now that I've seen this new way. Now as I see our new way of church becoming perhaps a little antiquated, when I see young new pastors starting churches "their" way, I find myself defensive and not so open. I am on the other side of the fence. Hmm. Experience matures, and I am maturing. And I have to admit, when I went into the chapel service the other week of a very traditional Presbyterian college, with its ornate stained-glass windows and dramatic organ music, I felt a certain closeness to God, and not at all a smug I-know-better attitude. I am maturing.

I count those years of elementary-school church to be some of the most exciting in the history of Bear Valley. Meeting in a school, and all that that involves is a wonderful experience. It is fun to set up and tear down with people you love. And it is fun to reach people who might not dare to set foot in a steeple-topped building but who would comfortably enter the doors of the school their third grade child attends. And it is fun to have people come and visit just because they've been there, done that at another place, and maybe they might want to help us out. Usually those are good, good people.

I do not drive by Bransford Elementary at Glade Road and Bransford Road, or O. C. Taylor Elementary on Pool Road, or Glenhope Elementary farther north on Pool Road, without thinking of how lives were changed there, and how a church had a home there.

While meeting in those schools our church offices, as I've said before, were on Harwood near Precinct Line Road. To this day I still meet people who remember our trailer out front in the parking lot that advertised Bear Valley Community Church.

By the way, we added the word "Community" at the time we dropped the word "Creek." We felt that the word "Community" helps express the goal of designing our Sunday morning worship time as an event for everyone in our community.

chapter 9

Bible for Dummies

> "The unfolding of your words gives light; it gives understanding to the simple."
> (Psalms 119:130 NIV)

The office on Harwood was special in many regards. Well, any place we had offices was a fun place, I do say. Seeing Wanda sitting at the desk, smiling when I walked in always made me feel good. There is something about having a gray-haired motherly figure sitting behind the secretary's desk that makes one feel secure somehow. And then, you could hear laughter often. With Keith Prather around, and Julie Zuefeldt and Jeff Clack, a spirit of camaraderie abounded. And with Sam, and then Sam and Lee Johnson at the helm of such a ship, a sense of wisdom and solid foundation was felt, as well as fun. Lots of meetings were held in the meeting room at that office location. I held my first "What the Bible is All About" Seminar. Now that was something really big on my part.

Here's the story: Sam and I were taking a day off in Dallas one day when he decided he wanted to go by The Heights Baptist Church in Richardson. Sam has always been interested in seeing how other churches do things.

Since I have known him, he has always been a learner. That particular day he wanted to see how The Heights new church building looked. The doors were open so we went in and walked around. I walked by the counter where there was a bunch of handouts and brochures. One really interested me. It was something like: "How to understand the Bible—from Genesis to Revelation…in one weekend." Wow. That was so intriguing. I knew that most of our members were brand new Christians who were Biblically illiterate. A course like that would be great for them. I would like it also. Well, anyone, I thought would be interested in such a course, surely. I picked up the brochure, eager to call the number listed on it and talk to the man who taught the course.

My eagerness to talk to the teacher of said course diminished as soon as I heard his voice on the other end of the line. I guess it was the southern drawl, or maybe the preacher-like, slow, patronizing tone of voice that comes with years of practicing a holier-than-thou attitude. (I got all that from his first "Yes?") I proceeded to ask him about the course. His answer made me realize that it would be the exact wrong thing for Bear Valley. "Well, ma'am, I give the background of the stories that everyone knows. You know, the background of people such as Noah, Abraham, John the Baptist, etc. And I bring it all together in a timeline that shows just how God brought His message to the world."

"The stories that everyone knows." I knew that man's "everyone" must just be church folk. And, of course it would be. It was being offered in a Baptist church, to church members. But some of my Bear Valley friends would not think of the name "Abraham" unless his last name is Lincoln, and they think of John the Baptist in the same way they think of Tom the Presbyterian. This man's course on understanding the Bible would presume knowledge of the Bible.

The culture of the traditional church is a culture. And it has a language of its own, and that language and culture are foreign to foreigners. Culture is an interesting thing. The ones who see it as a culture are the ones outside of it. Inside, it is "just the way things are" and always have been.

As young missionaries in Brazil, Sam and I got to see American culture as a "thing," something that is different from other cultures. That experience really helped me when we started Bear Valley, as I realized that church culture is just that—a culture.

"Culture Shock" became an expression we totally understood. I believe it would behoove most churches of today to have a study on just what "culture shock" a person might face when he/she comes into their worship services. It would be very similar to, say, my going to a synagogue, or even a Catholic mass. There are things they "do" that are understood by the locals…and so not understood by the foreigners. There are stories and anecdotes that the locals tell and understand.

Like the story of Moses: If it were not for the movie "Prince of Egypt," many would know nothing about him. And what about the folks who don't frequent movies? They would be up a creek.

I need to get back to my subject. I knew by talking to that man who was going to give the weekend course on the Bible that Bear Valley did not fit his lesson. Sad to say,

I think even in that traditional Southern Baptist church, his lesson would not fit many of the people who would venture to take his course. It would be like taking a beginner's computer class and finding out that before you came you were already supposed to know how to turn on the computer, and what the terms "log on," and "surf the net" meant. Prior knowledge was assumed.

I decided that I would tackle teaching the course myself. I would call it "What the Bible is All About," after Henrietta Mears' book of that same name. Whoa, I soon found out this self-assigned project was challenging, to say the least. I began reading everything I could on how to simply explain the Bible. I devoured Mears' book, which I found to be extremely educational, and inspirational as well. I also bought books that were what I call "seeker-sensitive:" <u>The Idiot's Guide to the Bible</u> and <u>Bible for Dummies</u>. They were great quick references, but I realized that both the quick references and Mears' book would be hard to handle in a mere weekend. What helped the most was <u>Max Anders' 30 Days to Understanding the Bible in 15 Minutes a Day</u>, recommended by dear Julie Zuefeldt whose small group was going through it at the time. What a find it was. It had charts, and fill-in-the blank statements that adapted themselves to my new course perfectly. I was excited.

I advertised my course as one where "Absolutely No Previous Knowledge of the Bible" would be required. The course would presume absolutely nothing. Well, I found out really soon just what "nothing" meant. It meant NOTHING.

I had just four students take the course. One was a (self-admitted) backslidden Baptist who had found Bear Valley when he and his wife wanted their children to start being raised in "the church." Another was a young lady who had been a nominal Episcopalian as a child, but did not remember anything she had learned, and was now hungering and thirsting for God. Another was reared in a Catholic home and had attended Catholic schools in the northeast all during her growing-up years. The other, a young college student, had no church background whatever, and was just wanting to know more about Christianity. All four of these people were delightful and eager to learn. I was delighted and eager to teach them.

During the break, after my introduction in which I stated that no prior Bible knowledge would be assumed, and that this may mean the course "might be too elementary for some of you," I found out just how elementary it needed to be. I found out I had assumed knowledge! I had said, "As you know, there are two parts to the Bible, the Old Testament and the New Testament." During that break, I learned that I should never say, "As you know." Two of those precious people did NOT know there were two parts to the Bible at all. This was a sorely needed education to me. One that every pastor of every church, including traditional, needs to learn: there are folks in congregations everywhere that do not know "beans about beans." They do not know what the numbers mean in references such as 2 Timothy 2:2, nor do they know even the importance of the Bible to the Christian faith. All this spoke not only volumes to me of the Biblical illiteracy of Americans today, but it also told me of how the words

"Jesus," "Holy Spirit," and even "God" were so misunderstood by people everywhere.

If for no other reason than to find out what "no prior Bible knowledge" means, that course was wonderful for me. It brought home to me just who we were trying to reach. Our job became mammoth, in importance and in content.

Since that first weekend of the "What the Bible is All About" seminar, I have changed the name to "Bible for Dummies" then settled on "Introduction to the Bible." That is a less demeaning title than one with the word "dummies" in it, for sure, and it clarifies it better than the broad "What the Bible is All About." I have also since made it a six-week course as part of Bear Valley Institute, which offers about four different courses for people who want to grow in their faith. Needless to say, it has been a fun experience, giving a thumbnail sketch of the Bible to folks who do not know "beans about beans."

Bear Valley Institute was a yearly event, usually during the summer, to give additional training to our leaders. We largely relied on the Institute, Retreats and Apprenticeship as the main methods of training our leadership.

chapter 10

Getting a Grip

> "Each one should test his own actions. Then he can take pride in himself, without comparing himself to somebody else..." (Galatians 6:4 NIV)

So after chasing that rabbit of church culture and how it should assume no Bible knowledge with lots of its folks, I come back to how Bear Valley and I were doing meeting in a school. I say "I" because this is my story, remember.

Even though meeting in a school and working in an office building were great, exciting, unique experiences in the onward movement of the kingdom of God, they did not measure well on my need-for-prestige marker. Every once in a while that need would rear its ugly head. Like when we'd go to Baylor Homecoming and someone would ask what we were doing with our lives. Starting a church that meets in a school sounded lame to me, so I would hope that Sam would elaborate on just what that meant, in the new-paradigm church movement. If he didn't start pontificating, I would. If the person did not know about the movement, then we, or I, would have to explain it, which maybe would take up too much time for said person. In that case we would get no respect. It would be just as if we were starting a church in a school because we couldn't find a church that would have us. Now is that thinking crazy or what?

I knew in my heart that God led us to start Bear Valley. I knew in my heart that seeing all those unchurched people come to Christ in the school, or the shopping center, or the movie theater was really what ministry was all about. It was what Jesus would do. But when it came to talking to an old Baylor friend who was a successful lawyer, doctor, or Indian chief, I felt like a failure. I would kick myself for even coming to homecoming, where fat people and failures don't show their faces.

My confessing my insidious need for respect is my way of slaying the demon of "image is everything." It is not everything. In fact it is nothing in God's eyes. And what a relief when we (I) discover that. It means I can let go of that striving for prestige and get on with my life.

I am happy to say that I have had an overall victory in that area. And it came before we moved into our building, which would have been my symbol for respect. Oh, the image-demon rears its ugly head now and again, but I am so learning how to bop it down. Hallelujah.

So the Bear Valley school days were good for me. They taught me humility, and to accept who I am. God uses many ways to teach me needed lessons.

Before we started meeting in the schools we bought property for a church building. Colleyville required that before you could rent school facilities for church services you had to prove that you owned land and had plans to build on it within two years. That was a given. Owning land was exciting. It meant a future…a future with stability. Even though I had learned—and am still learning—my lesson on respect and prestige, the idea of having our own building was exciting.

Everyone has his/her idea of what he/she wants in a church building. I am no exception. Fortunately I had been to counseling to work through my control issues so that I would not be insistent on getting my way. In fact, I forced myself to not be on the design committee. Of course I am always ready to not go to another committee meeting, but this was different. I had a vested—whatever that means—interest in this new construction. It was with great pride in my victory over not controlling the universe that I relinquished any dreams I had for our new, first facility. And that meant that no matter what I thought about the floor plans, etc., I had to keep my mouth shut. Now that subject—mouth—could be the fodder for a whole other book. Suffice it to say I have worked on my tendency to be "motor mouth." I have put to memory the verse Proverbs 10:19 and it has served me well: "When words are many, sin is not absent. He who holds his tongue is wise." If you are reading this and thinking that I have not mastered this besetting sin, my words to you would be, "just be thankful that I've learned what I have. Otherwise my mouth would be overflowing even more."

So I learned to keep quiet on my opinions on the new building. I'm afraid I didn't learn that lesson before we purchased the land. I was filled with ideas on good places to build. North Precinct Line Road in almost Keller was not one of them. Sam is so smart. He decided that location would be great, even if the road hadn't been finished and new buildings hadn't been built yet when we bought the land. He could see the potential…and knew the price was right.

Sam is such a brilliant man. This was also seen in whom he hired as the architect for our new building. Actually Sam is quick to tell you that the land and the choice of architect was a committee decision. That is true, but I'm tooting Sam's horn here. Somehow he found Jim Langford, a man who not only had incredible architectural skills but incredible insight into function and form representing a church's message. Constantly we were amazed at the lengths Jim went to understand Bear Valley and why we existed. I never knew architects did that kind of thing. It seemed every aspect of Bear Valley was an education for me.

The building design committee agreed with Langford's plans. There was an excitement that began spreading throughout the church. I don't remember if I said this or not, but when I refer to the "church" I refer to the people, obviously not the building. That's a big "duh" since we didn't have a building.

Soon we were going to get one. Pictures were taken on the site—of Jeff Clack in an earth-mover, Sam with his arms open wide where the auditorium was going to be, and others running around excitedly just to show the enthusiasm of, well, everyone. Oh, and that is not to mention the Vacation Bible School that was held under a big tent the summer before groundbreaking.

The picture on the cover is our first building.

chapter 11

Possess the Land

> "For we are God's fellow workers; you are God's field, God's building." (1 Corinthians 3:9 NIV)

When we were in the schools a couple came on board at Bear Valley that I would call a "Power Couple." And if you know them, you know that is exactly what they are.

Jonathan and Jennifer Howes were on the track to become church planters. Sam had been asked to coach Jonathan as he started a new church for college students near the University of Texas at Arlington. When Sam learned that Jonathan was planning on leaving that ministry, Sam quickly got permission from the sponsoring church to hire them at Bear Valley. While in seminary they wanted, as part of their education, to be involved in a church-start that had already started. Bear Valley, therefore, seemed the place to be…and glad we were (and still are) that they saw that, and came on board.

At first Jennifer was what we needed, in that she was a dynamic, enthusiastic go-getter children's director! One of her first jobs was to have a Vacation Bible School on our new property. We'd had Vacation Bible Schools before—in backyards of church members—(which would make another great chapter) but this would be the first time that all the workers and all the children would at the same place at the same time.

Jennifer had to rent a huge tent...and, of course, corral workers and kids...and, well, do it.

After the first night, which was cancelled(!) because of a thunderstorm, it went off great. Lots of new kids showed up. I was reminded again of who we were reaching, and how we couldn't assume anything. You see, I was the Bible story teacher for the fourth and fifth graders. The second night of VBS the lesson was on Paul. I asked the question: "Can anybody tell me what a missionary is?" I just knew that that was a dumb question, but I was going to ask it anyway, just to get the lesson started. No hand went up. "Anybody? What does a missionary do?" Still no hand. Finally one boy had his answer, "It's someone who is paid money to fight in a war." Whoa. He was the only one with an answer and he was talking about a mercenary, not a missionary! So I guess school vocabulary lists don't include "missionary." I would also find out that school vocabulary lists also don't include the word "disciple."

I was getting a lesson.

As I mentioned, we held many backyard Vacation Bible Schools before we had property or a building. During one of those times our little Jewish neighbor Nadine attended and got to memorize John 3:16, and John 14:6. She also got to play her violin when we had game time. Musical chairs with a live violin is fun.

Now back to the adventure of finally having our own building!

Always in building any edifice, the due date does not equal the move-in date. Weather, budget, slow construction workers, etc., etc., all equal to delay the move date to months from the given date. That only dampened our enthusiasm a little. We all knew that due dates meant practically nothing.

Finally, though, Mother's Day of 2000 was set as our opening…with the big Grand Opening (with mailers and all) to be the following fall, allowing the summer time to get the kinks out of the new facility. During this time, Sam began enlisting more staff to accommodate the projected influx of new people come fall.

To say it's a "long story" is really an understatement, but the hiring of Lee Johnson as a kind of co-pastor and Jonathan Howes as a kind of young adult pastor was a major stroke of genius on Sam's part. Here were two of the highest caliber people in the world joining forces with the highest caliber person, Sam, to bring Bear Valley into the 21st Century. We were poised to boom.

Lee was hired while we still met in the school. His first service was at O.C. Taylor Elementary School.

Jonathan was hired after we had been in the building for a while.

Sam remembers telling Jonathan that he (Sam) was able to pastor an average of 200, Lee added 200 more and Jonathan is expected to add 200 more. And we reached an average of 650 while Jonathan was with us! (This would have been more than a year after moving in the building.)

So boom we did. The building, plus new staff, plus keen mailers, brought all kinds of new folks to church that fall. By the beginning of the second service each week we would be out of donuts! Now that was my marker as to how well we were doing. Seriously, we were on a roll.

Right before we moved into the building Sam got Lee and Peggy Johnson to come on board.

Every once in a while you come across a couple that you register in your mind as the ideal couple. Now relegating anyone to the status of "ideal" sets him/her up to falling off your pedestal. Nobody's perfect, after all. Well, almost nobody. Both Lee and Peggy Johnson, even individually, come pretty near close, in my opinion. Now both of them would protest this paragraph. I can hear them now. "Nancy, we are so human, etc., etc." And that protest would even set them higher on that pedestal. "Precious people" is what I would call them.

I met Peggy some thirty-five years ago when she was a freshman at Baylor University. I had arrived there a year earlier with my twin, also named Peggy. I don't know how we met but when I think of Peggy Basden I think of a beautiful little blonde who would walk across campus smiling and saying "hello" to everyone. She became known around campus as a vibrant Christian young lady, and her sweet, happy demeanor was contagious. I didn't know her well, but my sister became very acquainted and the two Peggys even eventually led a Bible Study together at the Baptist Student Union building.

My recollection of Lee Johnson dates back to Baylor days as well. One afternoon my twin and I went to sing hymns at a local nursing home. We were to lead the music, sing a duet, and then hand the service over to someone who was going to preach the sermon. That someone was a black haired young Baylor student who impressed us with his gentle ways with those elderly folks. He didn't have a southern drawl but it turned out he was a Mississippi native. Peggy (my sister) and I always liked to meet Mississippi folk because we had lived there for three years as children, and felt an affinity with them. Though we did not know Lee well during those days, we knew he was a high caliber fella.

Years later when I found out that Lee Johnson and Peggy Basden had found each other and gotten married I thought, "Wow. What a great match." Little did I know that our lives would be intertwined through the years.

In seminary Sam and I and Lee and Peggy found ourselves together on mission endeavors to the Yucatan peninsula in Mexico. Sam's parents had visited the area on a vacation earlier; and, as they usually did on vacation trips to other countries, they made an appointment with the area Baptist missionary. Levi Price and his wife, Lou, and their children were living in Merida where Levi was working with churches and missions, trying to reach the Yucatan people for Christ. He took Nana and Daddy-Bob around to see the work there. They met local pastors and were touched by the financial need of God's work there.

When they got back home they contacted Dr. Justice Anderson, the missions professor at Southwestern Baptist Theological seminary, and asked him to get a group of seminary students together and plan a mission trip to Merida. The summer after we got married, Sam and I went to visit with Levi and the main pastor in Merida, Pastor Mandujano. When we came back we, and Dr. and Mrs. Anderson looked at the needs of the area that Levi Price, and Pastor Mandujano shared with us and formulated a plan to help them financially and personally. Lee and Peggy could tell here how they became part of the team, but suffice it to say, the Carmacks and the Johnsons continued our friendship through those three week mission trips to the Yucatan in the summers of 1979 and 1980. During the rest of the year, we spent time with Lee and Peggy on projects such as a revival in Malone, Texas. Sam had his first pastorate there and decided that that little church ("little" is the operative word: attendance usually ran about nine people) needed a weekend revival. He asked his now good friend, Lee Johnson, to come preach it. With Lee's preaching, and Sam leading the singing, that little church got revived. When we left the church to serve in Brazil as missionaries (another book, some day), the attendance was about seventeen. How exciting, and we could thank Lee and Peggy for helping almost double the size! In fact every stateside church Sam has pastored has grown by at least 50%… two doubled in size and Bear Valley grew from an average attendance of 5 to 650. Back to the Johnsons…

I can also thank Lee and Peggy for quiche and spinach salad. One evening they invited us over for supper at their new little seminary home. Lee and Peggy have always seemed to have a proper way about them. They just seem to know how to "do" things. I remember looking forward to seeing their home because I wanted to see how they decorated it and what they served to eat. I knew it would all be classy. Sure enough, the house had clever, pretty touches throughout. Their coffee table had magazines seemingly haphazardly placed on it. The very next week I noticed that was how Southern Living magazine had its coffee table "decorated." Classy. So what was for supper?

Quiche and spinach salad. I had never had either one before. How interesting to have an egg pie for the evening meal. And with a salad made of raw spinach. I was getting some culture! And it was delicious. That was some thirty years ago and still, to this day, when I eat quiche I think of where I first ate it.

Lee and Peggy and Sam and I all left seminary eventually and went our separate ways. We did keep in touch through Christmas cards. We knew that they had spent some time working with North Fort Worth Baptist Church. They moved to Durant, Oklahoma from there where Lee became associate pastor at the First Baptist Church. When you ask their daughter, Julia, where she was born she will say, "I was born in Texas, but my parents lived in Oklahoma." Durant is across the northeast Texas state line, which is the Red River. Peggy and Lee had to go to Sherman, Texas for the birth. Later the Johnsons crossed the Red River for good.

It was in 1991 that we got our friendship back in full swing. Lee was pastoring a relatively new church in southwest Fort Worth, McCart Meadows Baptist Church. Though he hadn't started the church he had become its pastor not long after it started. When Sam began thinking that the Fort Worth area was where he wanted to plant his own church, he contacted Lee. Lee was full of ideas. Come to find out, he and his church had also been learning the ways of Saddleback Church in California and Chicago's Willow Creek Church before we had. As soon as we moved to our apartment in Bedford, we drove down to McCart Meadows Church and attended a Saturday night service. It was awesome. I had only attended one out-of-the-box church by then, and that was in sunny California where lots of things are out-of-the-box. Here in Texas we were seeing one in action. The fact that it was on a Saturday night made it feel even better.

Lee walked in wearing a casual white shirt with the name and logo of the church. How cool was that. When Peggy appeared she was flanked by young women and they all were wearing Saturday-type clothes. No Easter parade here.

The auditorium was so un-sanctuary-like. No pulpit. No choir loft. There weren't even any pews, just chairs. It felt very comfortable and I could picture myself in a church like this of my own. The music was contemporary which was refreshing. When Lee started preaching I hardly felt I was listening to a sermon because there was no shouting. He was talking to us, and with us. This church felt like a living example of what we had heard about at Rick Warren's church the previous summer. It got me excited about the adventure God and Sam were leading me on.

After the service Lee and Peggy invited us to go eat at a new restaurant called Chili's. I remember expecting all kinds of chili on the menu. Years before they had introduced me to quiche and spinach salad. Now they were getting ready to introduce me to another new delicacy: the Awesome Blossom. I've decided that Lee and Peggy know what's yummy to eat.

As we started Bear Valley and would come across typical problems a new church-start has (Sam will write that book some day), Sam and Lee would get together and commiserate. As for Peggy, we'd meet on occasion as well and talk girl talk. After we'd been a church for a few years

I started thinking it would be fun to have a women's retreat. The first and only speaker that I thought of was Peggy Johnson. I got on the phone, found out when she could do it, and then scheduled the retreat. It was great. The women loved her. Since then she has been the main speaker at many of our women's retreats. Why try and improve on perfection?

At that first women's retreat Peggy shared with the ladies how she found her calling in life. As a teenager she had been drawn to thoughts of the ministry. Typically women preachers were not thought well of in Baptist churches. She got her seminary degree and knew that some day God would lead to just the right path. As I recall it was at a Quick Stop where she happened to look down at a newspaper and, well, the rest is history. She is now a chaplain at Cook Children's Hospital in Fort Worth. Anyone who knows Peggy knows that those sick children and their parents are blessed indeed to have her as their chaplain. Currently she is working with little cancer patients there.

Let's move on a few years. If we don't, it will take as long to read this book, as it was to live it! Back to the church, and more specifically the new church building.

Sam was knowing he needed some help, if a church building was going to mean we were to reach more people for Christ. To be able to minister to new folks, new staff was a necessity. Always the problem in finding staff is making sure the said staff member understands the culture in which he will work. Some staff members we've hired in the past did not "get it." They were encumbered by a traditional mindset. The who-is-right game would be played out and only frustration by both parties would be the result. Sam knew he had to be careful.

After much thought and prayer Sam kept coming to Lee Johnson's name. Sam gave him a call. They met at one of Sam's and my most special eating-places, in the Worthington Hotel in downtown Fort Worth. They have a great lunch menu with not too expensive prices. And they had these booths that are secluded where you can meet and talk and no one can eavesdrop. It was there that Sam approached Lee with the idea of coming on board at Bear Valley. I have to say that when Sam told me that he was going to talk to Lee about that subject, I thought, "Nah, that would be too good to be true. Forgetaboutit." But when Sam came home from that lunch meeting, he was all smiles. Lee WOULD think and pray about it. In fact, Lee said that he was already sensing that God might want to move him to another church. Wow. "Wow" was all I could say. I did not want to get my hopes up.

Fast forward—my hopes got up and have stayed up. Lee and Peggy came on board right before we moved into the building on Precinct Line. Talk about exciting times.

After Lee and Peggy left McCart Meadows Church, much to the dismay of its members, and moved to a home in Hurst and settled in at Bear Valley, the church started to grow.

A little before this time the Howeses came along. Sam had met Jennifer and Jonathan at a church planters' assessment retreat in which Sam was one of the assessors, and Jennifer and Jonathan were two of the "assessees." Sam came home from that retreat incredibly impressed with that couple. Since we needed a children's director right away, he approached Jennifer for the job. She took it, and as Sam had wanted, her highly creative, funny, enthusiastic-as-well husband eventually came on board, too. There for a while we had Sam, Lee and Jonathan as the teaching pastors. Oh my. Each of them, by themselves, was incredible. When you put them together, planning services and other events in the church, our growth was almost setting records. In our church building we were having over 600 people attending three services. That same sized church building was only supposed to accommodate 300, so of course we couldn't have just one service. Two services on Sunday was typical for churches around the area, but we wanted to reach folks who worked on Sunday, so we also added a Saturday evening service… Exciting times, indeed. Oh, and we hadn't exceeded the fire marshal code for occupancy…yet, anyway.

Now in any new facility anywhere there are some "kinks" (I can't think of a better word). And everything is not going to please everybody. When folks would come up to me and say, "Nancy, why didn't we put in a proper kitchen?" I would shrug my shoulders and reply, "I know. It's a shame. I guess I should have been on the design committee after all." That became my standard response. I've learned through the years that explanations were usually pointless, like, "We didn't have enough money. If you would have given more, we could have had a top-rate, fully-equipped church building. It's all your fault." 'Course that was not an explanation but a yearning-to-be-said shame statement that my memory verse on when-words-are-many-sin-is-not-absent kept me from saying.

So we were in our building. We had momentum. Life was good. People were coming out of the woodwork to find out about this new-fangled church. With the new people, though, many of them longtime Christians, came new expectations. Some of those unmet expectations caused these new visitors not to stay. Some stayed and began to let their desires be known: "we need a longer praise and worship set," "we need more old hymns sung in the service," "we need more traditional-style sermons," "we need more nutritious breakfast food, not just donuts and coffee," "we need to get to know the pastor as our closest friend," etc., etc. We found that people who had not been raised in church nor had attended church in a very long time, if ever, had no such expectations. "Low-expectation people" are really easy to have around. Not so sometimes with high-expectation folks. They can be a challenge, especially to people pleasers like myself. I was beginning to see why some churches never really want to grow. It is more comfortable being with family, where you know just what is expected.

Sam is clever. When some of those high expectation folks would voice their complaints, Sam would listen but would somehow make known that (though not in these words) "this is not your grandfather's church." Lee is clever also. When those folks would say things should be "such and such," his pat answer was, is, "Now, that's an idea!" Accompanied by a nod and a smile, it would soothe most suggestion-givers. Both Sam and Lee are famous at Bear Valley for echoing Rick Warren's response to new ideas, "That's a great idea. Why don't YOU do it?"

With some folks, like me, that empowered us! (Yes, I admit, I can be one of those high expectation people that I complain about.)

This next chapter will tell of an example of myself being empowered.

chapter 12

School of Rock

> "...let's just go ahead and be what we were made to be, without enviously or pridefully comparing ourselves with each other, or trying to be something we aren't." (Romans 12:6 Message)

One day, in the spring of 2004, in our family room, Will started watching the DVD of the movie SCHOOL OF ROCK. It was not a movie I was particularly interested in, not being a huge Jack Black fan and all. I had some time on my hands, though, so I decided to watch it with Will. Little did I know that I would get "hooked." The movie was great...and made me rethink my lack of love for Jack Black. AND my brain started brainstorming: Why couldn't WE do our own School of Rock?!

I mentioned it to Will, and he gave a hesitant nod. That didn't deter me. One thing I know about myself: when I get motivated I get motivated!

Many things came together to make the timing perfect. Will and Laura were in high school and they had the skills we needed, and their friends did, too. Also, I had just "taken" Scott Houston's course on HOW TO PLAY THE PIANO IN A FLASH on PBS. I took it because

I was curious as to how he approached teaching the piano in a flash, and when I watched it I realized he was teaching chords, and everything one would need to just play keys in a band.

We decided that Bear Valley's School of Rock would be one night a week for ten weeks. We'd start in June and end with a big concert in August. We'd teach guitar, bass guitar, drums, keyboard, and vocals. We'd also have great snacks every week. Besides teaching some music I wanted the goal to be: HAVE FUN!! Oh, and the only students we wanted were middle school students!! I've always had an affinity towards that age group (probably because most people don't) and I knew that age group would be interested in learning how to play in a rock band.

So we started. We first had a meeting with the parents to let them know what was expected of their kids…which really was not much, other than a good attitude. If their child had an instrument, great; if not, that was okay.

At every meeting before we'd divide up into our classes, we'd first have a guest "speaker" who would talk to the group about stage presence, stage fright, or whatever he/she thought an up and coming rock star would need to know. etc. Our assistant music man, Scott Norman, was one of those great speakers.

Also, Sophia Staecker Studer, was awesome at showing the kids how to work a crowd.

Laura was our master of ceremonies each meeting as well as our administrator. She kept tabs on attendance, and just did all the detail work involved. Plus, she helped out in the voice class. She has sung solos in public throughout her life, and is great at that.

Will was in charge of the guitar and bass guitar class. He brought some of his own guitars from home for those who didn't have them. (Most of the kids brought their own.) His goal was to teach them four or five chords that are common in most songs. We picked out a few songs to do—so as to get ready for the concert—which, of course, included those guitar chords. Who helped teach those classes were Brett Wittman and Alex Bargsley.

Allison Launius, Jenny Travis Campbell, Bailey Jo (Swanzy) Carmack and Laura were the vocal coaches. Their goal was to teach their students not just how to sing (sustain notes, keep pitch, etc.), but how to hold a mic, "work the mic" and whatever else you do when you're the lead singer.

I taught the keyboard class. The very first night I realized that my method had some drawbacks. I thought using Scott Houston's "How to Play the Piano in a Flash" would be the key to getting those kids to play "in a flash." Well, I needed an overhead video camera for that like the one he used, so I could "show" how the chords were played. Otherwise, it would have so worked. (If you're interested in Houston's course, I HIGHLY recommend it—as a one-on-one course....not for a class, though.)

The percussion class was led by Jan Boling, Bear Valley's own drummer. She got Justin Cartlidge and Marcus Hatcher really drumming!!

The highlight of the ten week course was the concert! Invitations were sent out to family and friends and the auditorium was full! The goal was for each kid to experience a rock star atmosphere in a concert. Before each guest walked into it, they were encouraged to make signs for their rock stars. Some signs were already made: like, "You rock, Ian!!!"; "I love you, Stefan!"; "I'm Swooning, Ryan!!"; "Way to Go, Kourtney!!" etc. Each band member had their own set of signs made, and their family and friends made even more.

The key for a successful concert was mixing the new players with experienced players. That allowed a brand new guitar player to experience the fun of being on stage in a rock concert.

As I recall there were two bands made up of these middle school students. They all came into the auditorium together at the first, to the "We Will Rock You" song by QUEEN, being played on the sound system, wonderfully run by Greg Bargsley. Well, you can imagine the excitement in the audience. Cigarette lighters were already lit and raised. And signs were waved. And I, the director, was—and clearly still am—VERY enthused!

Hmm. This makes me wonder why I haven't done another School of Rock. Oh yeah, that was a special time...when I had a special cast of characters: teachers, and students, and parents. If someone wants to do another, you can call me, and I'll give you some pointers. (I'm not getting any younger, so I'll let YOU do it.)

So I considered that out-of-the-box middle school School of Rock a success.

It wasn't the only Rock being played at Bear Valley on other days than Sunday. Pretty soon Rob was scheduling Christian rock concerts, with professional bands. The first was an ambitious endeavor, booking a nationally known band, an up and coming band that would bring lots of young people to Bear Valley. And it did. There was fever pitch excitement all around. On the local radio stations around, advertisements were bellowed out across the Metroplex. A concession stand as well as a t-shirt and CD booth were artistically planned. Rob was running around with more gusto than usual.

The big day brought more excitement...and frustration. It turns out that all Christian rock bands don't necessarily act Christian. I won't mention the name of the band, but its members definitely gave those of us who had close contact with them a kind of disillusionment, shall we say.

Ah, but every other concert we had was FANTASTIC. And Rob had many. And he always knew just how to promote them, and produce them. And our new building was the perfect venue for those concerts.

For one thing it wasn't your normal-looking church building. Well, that was the whole idea behind its look. And it was getting some buzz. When I would invite people to it and tell them where it was, they would say, "Oh, that weird looking building? My friend and I were wondering what that was going to be."

It's easy to invite folks to a place that is safe, where there are few expectations. Nowadays a lot of churches have followed suit and become comfortable places for anybody and everybody. Starbucks came up with a clever label for this type of building. They call it "The Third Place." "There's home," they say, "and work and we all need a "third place" for regrouping." And that's what we at Bear Valley want people to experience, a type of "third place."

That, of course, has not followed without criticism. Some people think that this new-fangled church (whose "type" has now been going on for over 30 years) is just a phase. And that respect for God will come back, which includes dressing up to show reverence, and soft, quiet, "holy" music will resume. I don't know about that...but I do believe that Jesus would approve of Bear Valley. That's not to say that he disapproves of First Denominational Church down the road, but in this day and age, where people don't want to be labeled, and categorized, well, a community church is an easier draw than the denominational church. I'm just sayin'.

Churches like ours have been criticized because we sometimes use the marketing approach to reach people. Well, if that were all we were using, well, I'd be the first to criticize. We just want to be smart, and know where people are at. It is through MUCH prayer that we see that only if we KNOW folks, will we be able to (prayerfully) reach them.

For a while (really many years) we used a very effective mailer called THE TOP TEN REASONS TO AVOID CHURCH. It was at a time when David Letterman was becoming well known. We had scores of people coming to Bear Valley because they resonated with that mailer.

Basically, we simply tried to identify with people's frustrations about the church.

> **10. It's so BORING.** We include dramas, multimedia, upbeat music and humor. We don't make you listen to organ music or sing a bunch of old songs.

9. They want my MONEY. We encourage our guests not to give to the church. We want our service to be our gift to you, so leave your wallet at home.

8. The kids will HATE it. Your kids will have a blast. We have simultaneous programs on Sunday for all ages—safe, positive and fun place for children.

7. It takes ALL day. We don't think church should be an endurance test. You can come at 9:45 or 11:15, and we're out in about an hour. You will still have plenty of time to enjoy the day—hopefully relaxing.

6. Sermons are GUILT trips. We have practical, positive Bible teaching dealing with real issues: anger, worry, family, etc.

5. They'll EMBARRASS me. You can blend in with the crowd and remain anonymous for as long as you like. We let you check us out instead of vice versa.

4. I hate wearing TIES. We dress casually. Our goal is not to impress each other, just to get to know each other.

3. They're always BUGGING me. Some people like having strangers drop by at their home unannounced—most of us don't! At Bear Valley we promise not to visit you unless you specifically ask.

2. I don't UNDERSTAND. We teach in plain English and provide you with "Bear Notes" to help follow along.

1. Free COFFEE & TEA. Okay, so we could only think of nine reasons, but we do have espresso drinks and free coffee, tea, and Krispy Kreme donuts, not exactly a gourmet meal, but at least your stomach won't be rumbling!

Good marketing is difficult. This piece worked very well in the late 90's. We initially wrote it as ten positive reasons to attend church, thankfully we switched to a negative mode which touched a cord in many people's heart. I believe that best marketing strongly identifies with the desires of the recipient.

Direct mail still works in our area, but the internet has opened new avenues. Now the most effective marketing tool for Bear Valley is the Click Ads on a Google search. It's a little complicated, but you can set up rules so that your church appears when someone types in the search field and the words "Church" and "Your Town." Follow this up with an up-to-date, appealing website with service samples, clear directions to the church, but no donation button (hide it somewhere or send it out as an email to a safe list).

I would stay away from marketing companies. You should, yourself, become an expert in your area, they are not. Be skeptical of your own opinion. Create a focus group of your intended audience and test everything with them. Oh yes, use a mailing company when doing mass mailing, and give plenty of time for the post office to process your permit request. Also don't give them money for postage until the day of the mailing. The Post Office is rather bad about sending it out too early.

Numerous times folks would tell us that they kept that mailer on their fridge for weeks before they decided

School of Rock

to check us out. We really found that amazing, because, well, how many times do you really look at flyers labeled "resident" that come through the mail? By the way, churches throughout the country have used our Top Ten Reasons List often with great success.

We've also been criticized because we try to reach people with a "felt-needs" approach. Our goal was to have at least one practical "take away" in every sermon for every attender, even for the non-Christian. This meant the sermon needed to take into account the felt-needs of the listener. Then as they began to trust the wisdom of the Bible, they would be open to explore their real need, which is a relationship with Jesus Christ.

We assume that most of our visitors are skeptical about the Bible, so we generally would not start from a Bible verse, instead we would teach TOWARD a Bible verse. I would usually share a story from my life demonstrating a practical truth. Then turn to the Bible and in essence say, "Oh look. This has already been included in the Bible!" ...and then teach that passage or tell that Bible story.

Sometimes we would need to teach on a point which might be difficult for a non-Christian to hear, like tithing. I would preface that moment by saying something like, "This next point is for Christians only. It only works for those who have put their faith in Christ. If you are not a Christian, you probably should not do this since it only works when walking in the Spirit of God; but you need to hear this to give you some idea of what your life will be like if you trust Christ."

Above all, we tried to avoid manipulating people with guilt or shame. I believe it's the job of the Holy Spirit to convict. Our job is to tell our story and His story. Guilt and shame are powerful motivators, but they are not lasting motivators. The power of the Gospel is rooted in loving community with lots of grace.

Now this all makes me think of our missionary time in Brazil and how cultures can be vastly different. In Brazil, at least back in the early 1980's, it was socially acceptable to talk about one's faith while out in the marketplace. The Brazilians that we came to know (and love) were very open about everything, really. "How much did you pay for that car?" they might ask. Or they might say, "My, but you're looking like you've gained some weight." And just as easily they might ask, "Are you a believer in Christ Jesus, and do you know if you're going to heaven when you die?" (even if they'd just met you.)

Well, you can tell that here in the good ole USA people don't normally talk that way. Here in the good ole USA we need to be sensitive at how people communicate. I, personally, am turned off by street preachers, say, in downtown Fort Worth. However, Sam at times would BE a street preacher in Teresina, Piaui, Brazil, where we served a while as missionaries in the early '80's.

In closing, I would say that I believe Bear Valley did—and does—what Jesus would do in "doing church." Well, if I didn't think that I wouldn't have wanted to be a part of such excitement.

Jesus walked with the normal folks of his day. He would walk with (and does walk with) the folks of today. He talked (talks) with them. He spoke (speaks) their language. Would that we would do so today…all over the world.

chapter 13

All Over the World

> "Go therefore and make disciples of all the nations," (Matthew 28:19 NKJV)

While we're talking about "all over the world," Bear Valley has been instrumental in helping churches with similar visions start throughout the Metroplex, particularly Tarrant County. Sam has met with numerous church planters through the years, offering suggestions, telling of mistakes he's learned along the way, as well as having Bear Valley financially support church-starts. And some of those church starts started more churches.

Among them Fellowship of the Parks, Keller, Texas; Centerpoint Church, North Richland Hills, TX; Graystone Church, Loganville, GA. These three churches had a combined attendance on Easter, 2012, of 7,500. It would be safe to assume that of the churches which Bear Valley helped and the churches they helped, this number would be well over 10,000. I would think more than one-third of these attenders would have little or no church culture.

These churches would be great churches even without our modest help. Here's the point: what a joy to be a part of what God is doing in the whole world! Everyone associated with Bear Valley should have a deep sense of connectedness to God's plan when reading thank you notes such as these:

> I am indebted to Bear Valley Community Church for their investment in me and our church. I attended one of the early theater services where I experienced church in a new way. This was inspiring and helped me better visualize the church God had called me to plant. Sam almost immediately became my primary encourager and mentor. Bear Valley became a model for our plant to learn from and follow. Our start was difficult to say the least, but Sam and BVCC believed and supported... I cannot count the times I have gotten counsel, received administrative & staff support from Bear Valley, or borrowed something—and usually returned it late.
>
> —Doug Walker, Fellowship of the Parks

Here's another...

> Bear Valley had a huge impact on my life and ministry. As a young pastor and church planter Sam mentored me. The biggest thing I learned from Bear Valley is how to create a church service and environment to reach the unchurched. At Graystone, the church Jennifer and I started 8 years ago, we have had over 10,000 first-time visitors fill out "communication cards." We have seen about 500 people baptized. Bear Valley is having a huge impact in Atlanta, Georgia and beyond. I consider Graystone Church to be an extension of Bear Valley Community Church. I recently mentored a young pastor from our church, and we

> sent him and his launch team to start a church in Wilmington, VT (Valley Town Church). Vermont is the most unchurched state in the USA. They had 45 people in attendance on Easter Sunday (It was the largest church attendance within the 3 closest cities.) and have already seen someone far from God come to salvation in Christ. The church in Vermont is only one example of dozens and dozens of churches around the US and world that are a part of the Bear Valley Legacy.
>
> —Jonathan Howes, Graystone

From the getgo Bear Valley has been about missions. The dictionary definition of "mission" is a "ministry commissioned by a religious organization to propagate its faith or carry on humanitarian work." Often we think of missions as going far away, to distant lands…and we did do that. It also can be quite close, as in downtown Fort Worth, or in neighborhoods close by, and we did that as well.

In the past, the Church tended to delegate mission works to organizations. Today, the Church needs to involve its members in mission work. We do this because of God's calling in our life; however, without this, we lose our credibility with the non-Christian world. How can we "sit on our hands" when so many people around us are suffering? That is a very fair question the non-Christian asks us as we overly invest in the worship hour to the exclusion of the work week (missions).

In the "close by," I want to credit Michael and Melissa Hatcher for showing us how to do that. Michael and Melissa are an interesting couple. Michael was born and reared in El Paso, Texas, where he learned to speak fluent Spanish. In fact, I heard that he thought he was hispanic until he moved to east Texas where he got a basketball scholarship at East Texas Baptist University. That's when he learned he was indeed black, as in African American! I hope he didn't learn the hard way, because I think that east Texas can be more prejudiced than El Paso. Anyway, it was there in Marshall at ETBU that he met the love of his life, beautiful Melissa. Since she is white, caucasian, anglo, well, they have four children that look to Sam and me as if they are Brazilian, which translates "beautiful."

Michael has worked with the homeless for years near downtown Fort Worth, off of Lancaster Street. It was with that work, and his membership at Bear Valley (and previously Lee and Peggy's church in southwest Fort Worth, McCart Meadows Baptist Church) that he came up with the idea of the Lighthouse church, which became Bear Valley's inner city mission.

This is a totally unique church in that it reaches out to the homeless and down and out.

Lighthouse was truly unique in its early days. It met in (on) a vacant lot. No roof, no walls, no windows. There were chairs (donated by BVCC folks) AND there was a door! It was set up and everyone who attended walked through it (well, unless they sneaked in on the side).

Now Lighthouse has a wonderful building, Life House. Michael is director of that, where he mentors and case manages men who live there; men who have been separated from their parents or wives and children and are looking to get on their feet and reconcile with their families. They must be drug free for at least six months.

Some of them are coming straight from jail. He also runs Lighthouse Services, which provides ID's and birth certificates for the needy.

It should be said that Michael raises his own salary and has for several years now. As Melissa says, "God has miraculously and faithfully provided for our family all of these years!"

As for Melissa, she worked for years (until 2010) at Cornerstone Assistance Network in Fort Worth.

Melissa has now started a women's ministry, speaking and writing, etc. She also volunteers as the women's ministry director at Bear Valley and leads the "Breakfast Club" for youth age girls every Saturday morning.

Here's how Michael puts it:

> In 2001, God gave me a vision. I was then working as a case manager for a social service. As I gazed out the window of my office on the second floor of the Day Resource Center for the Homeless in Fort Worth, my eyes saw homeless people, but my heart saw lost and dying brothers and sisters. ...in need of a home, yes, but even more so in need of a Savior. You see, in the inner city of Fort Worth there are programs to help the street people find housing, here are shelters where they can sleep at night, there are places where they can find a meal, but nowhere on those dark streets will you find a church. No church in the community...no church for the community. Of course churches come with good intentions, handing out sandwiches and blankets. But a sandwich will not give life to the lost soul, a comfortable blanket will not cover sins. That day the Lord

spoke to my heart, "This is where you will build my church."

I was not called to start a church in the inner city because I was qualified, in fact my talents or resume had nothing to do with God calling me. I just simply said, "Lord, send me." For those God calls, He equips. Through Bear Valley Community Church God equipped me with everything I would possibly need to build His church in the inner city. Pastor Sam Carmack took me under his wing, discipled me, and taught me the important do's and don'ts of effective leaderships. Pastor Lee Johnson, my long time mentor, and the entire church body of Bear Valley encouraged me through prayer and financial contributions.

Lighthouse Community Church started in the inner city of Fort Worth. The grass was our carpet, the sky our ceiling and the honking buses our choir. Ours was a church without walls, quite literally. This church made of human bricks was specifically ordained to serve and unconditionally love the homeless, drug dealers, addicts, and prostitutes—the outcast of society. Still, while we ministered to the destitute and despairing souls on the streets, the Lighthouse became known as a beacon shining brightly in the darkness.

I have come to realize that without Bear Valley's support and encouragement, my vision of an inner city church would be just another daydream, a forgotten gaze out the window, watching those who were in need of a home, but even more so in need of a Savior.

-Michael Hatcher

All Over the World

In writing this book I emailed Amanda Gutierrez, asking her to tell me of her experiences with Bear Valley Missions. Her reply was so good, that I decided to just copy and paste it here. I couldn't improve on her words, plus this will let you get to know Amanda yourself (if you don't already have that privilege). This represents a lot of people at BVCC. I only inserted parenthetical explanations, where I thought they might be needed.

> I have to be honest when I say that I didn't want to go help in Mexico. My aunt from south Texas would bug me about going to help in Mexico. I would tell her, "Just because I am Mexican doesn't mean that I want to help other Mexicans." ...God has a GREAT sense of humor. I guess when I say something out loud and mean it, he is quick to change my mind and heart. I loved being in Mexico to help with VBS. It was fun being with the kids and helping them with crafts and hearing their laughter. I didn't understand them and most didn't understand me but that didn't stop us from having a good time together. The language barrier didn't prevent me from doing what I wanted to do. I was able to give hugs and smiles to those who wanted it and accepted it. I was able to sit beside a kid and just start helping when they needed it and it was accepted. I made friends with Paulina and David who I still communicate with today. Paulina recently married in March of 2011 and I was able to attend her wedding as a special guest.
>
> The next greatest experience in Mexico was being able to deliver shoeboxes that were filled with toys for the kids. To see the smiles and

happiness on all the kids' faces was an amazing experience. There is an orphanage that we visit and most times they have to share everything. They share clothes, socks, shoes and toys. When we come and bring gifts, the shoeboxes are labeled with each individual kid's name on it. So when the child receives his/her very own box with his very own name on it, that gift belongs to him only. That is the one item they don't have to share. Most don't open their boxes in front of others. Most will wait until everyone receives their gifts and then they will take to their rooms or a private area so they can open them by themselves. The few that do, stay with us and it's an awesome experience to see them open their gifts and get excited about what they received.

Going to be honest again I didn't want to go to India...

So here we are now jumping on the bandwagon to go to India. I didn't know anything about India. It didn't sound appealing to me and it definitely wasn't part of my plan but I had been raising all this money (for a trip to Romania with Echo Bible Church, which was canceled) and had been sending letters to those who were supporting me financially and prayerfully that I could not, not go. I was stuck! Once again, God always knows what he is doing. Thankfully most times his plans are better than my own plans. He knew all along that I would fall in love with the people of India and my heart would forever be in Hyderabad. India is so very different then the States. It's dirty and over-populated with not only motorcycles (and scooters) but with people, too. It's also very loud! Honking is non-stop and the honk is more of an I-am-here-just-in-case-you-didn't-see-me and not an angry honk. I remember having a headache at the end of first full day there and just wanted everything to be quiet! Most are very excited to meet Americans. I was taking pictures of people and buildings around me but there were also Indians taking pictures of us, too. I personally believe we were treated with respect everywhere we went and didn't meet a stranger either.

Bear Valley supports a home at a village in the middle of nowhere. There are about 35 residents that live at this home and it's mixed between kids and adults and about half have the AIDS virus. This home was founded by a lady named Yadema. She has a rocky past and wasn't a Christian until she was an adult. She had believed in other gods but she finally sought out the one true God and has been a faithful believer ever since. She didn't know how to read and after becoming a Christian she was blessed with being able to read and has read the Bible to its entirety several times now. Yadema has a passion for God and wants to help as many as she can. She started taking in orphans in her home but then there were so many and not enough space. She would find places for them to live but then the communities would kick them out once they found out some kids were infected with the AIDS virus or had parents with it. Only by God alone Bear Valley would come at the right time for this family to stay together. In December 2007, we helped them purchase their land. This would secure them a home and no one could ever make them move again. We also helped find water on their land and build a well. In 2010, the next step was to get them a fence since they had crops on their land now with having water, now that we had to watch for wild animals. We had taken clothes for all the kids in 2007 but that was hard to do. We had to take extra luggage and left some (of the luggage) there to haul all the clothes. So we decided to ask for donations during our Christmas Eve service. Here comes the blessings all over again. BVCC family came through and we had enough money to buy all the kids clothes but we were also able to buy all the women Sarees. So awesome how a group comes together when there is a need for others and not just others but those who are literally around the world.

I definitely look forward to this trip each year. It's only by the grace of God that I am allowed to make this journey. Only through Him I am able to have the funds to travel and have a great group of friends and family who support me in this journey as well. I have become friends with many in India. I am able to keep in touch with them through email and Facebook. God definitely knew what he was doing when plans fell through with Romania and we had to shift towards India. I had no idea that my life would be filled with such great friends such as Deepthi, Bernice, Ebby, Joseph, Hannah, Yadema and David. In 2010 I lost my mother. I received so much support from my Indian friends. Bernice and Ebby had traveled to the states for church business and some personal travel as well. Bernice told me that she didn't want to make the trip because the travel is hard on her but she knew I needed her during my grieving process. She wanted to be here with me to love me and show she was here for me. I can't tell you how much that meant to me. The expense is so great to travel to the States and the travel is not easy and to know that she had me in mind when making her final decision made my heart melt. Only God knew these plans and knew I would need her friendship to guide me through those hard times. While in India, our friends at the village also shared with me how they prayed for me and were very sorry for my loss.

I am honored and humbled each time I am able to make a mission trip. These trips are not about me but only about God and his plans for me. I have no expectation when traveling and when meeting new people. I want to always show kindness even to those I cross paths with here at home. You never know how you can impact someone else's life with the smallest gesture. A smile or hello can make a world of difference even when you aren't trying to make a difference. I never thought I would be used to help glorify God but it seems that God is always full of nice surprises. —Amanda

You can see why we wanted to just let Amanda tell you her story, in her way What an inspiration she is! I want to encourage you to lead your church to pick out two places in the world, one close, the other far; and continue to return year after year. It will help your own church and have a chance to leave a lasting impact on others.

I also hope you develop a place for interns. All of our interns were very effective. Scott Norman's musical talent gave us such a lift. He has since served very large churches taking the craft acquired at Bear Valley of creating a service which reaches skeptics. Jeff and Kim Cruse were instrumental in creating a hunger for world ministry. They now serve as missionaries in the Philippines. They started our international ministry. Jason McReynolds became our best video editor. Something he effectively used in a church he started in New Orleans, LA.

In conclusion…

Nowadays there are a lot of churches that seem similar to Bear Valley. Bear Valley was one of the first…and it is my belief that Bear Valley was unique in that it didn't (doesn't) just have contemporary music…and doesn't just offer folks a place to dress casually. Lots of churches now do that. It is more than the music and the attire. It is a conscious, and conscientious, focus on the person who is seeking answers to life's questions; the religiously curious, but not convinced.

It is not for the Christian. But, you ask, how will the Christian get "fed" if the talks on Sunday morning are not mainly for him/her? The answer? Small groups. Small groups where the Bible is studied, where prayer requests are made and prayed for, and where the Lord's Supper can be partaken. And yet, even in those small groups, the new believer, or even not-yet believer, can find safety, and warmth, and where his/her questions can be answered.

Hindsight is always 20/20, as they say. I can say that's true, now that I've lived and seen Bear Valley from its beginning…and am watching it move ever forward.

I saw it when it was a new, weird thing. The newest type of church in the area. Some called it "refreshing," others called it "disturbing." But now that there are churches like it all over the place it has gained credibility. That's meant it has lost its uniqueness, which makes me kind of sad. I liked being different. But what makes me glad is that Bear Valley's vision to reach folks that totally were turned off by tradition has found a kinship with so many churches now.

chapter 14

A New Chapter

> "In the last days, God says, I will pour out my Spirit on all people. Your sons and daughters will prophesy, your young men will see visions, <u>your old men will dream dreams.</u>" (Acts 2:17 NIV)

In 2003 I shocked my staff, telling them it was time for me to step down as Senior Pastor of the church. Here's what was going on: I knew that to take the next big step would require restructuring the staff. I did not have the emotional energy to face this. This was a whole new experience for me. I had always been a person with drive, passion and perseverence.

Instead of resigning I decided to take an extended leave-of-absence. During this time I recovered the emotional energy to lead. I returned to the church and led a long-term strategic planning group from which came the plans of the next building. We drew up a floor plan, organized a giving campaign and raised $900,000 in cash and pledges. The building eventually cost 1.6 million dollars.

After finishing the giving campaign, the lack of emotional energy returned. I realized I didn't have the drive to effectively lead a growing church, so in 2005 I stepped down as Senior Pastor of BVCC. I also had a deep desire to return to academic studies and try to grasp a clearer intellectual understanding of the changes in culture and church structure. I spent two years updating my academics, spending a good amount of time in Europe.

A few weeks after resigning I became very sick. It would take me almost three hours to get ready in the morning because of extreme muscle pain.

After months of this, finally I discovered the cause. It basically was the mistreatment of hypothyroidism. The lack of emotional energy was actually a form of depression. It was wonderful to have my life back, but to this day I deeply miss leading Bear Valley Community Church. Of course I believe that all of this was within God's providence, and it was time for someone else to take the reins of Bear Valley Community Church. Hopefully I can help others develop conversion-growth churches through teaching, writing and consulting.

Recently I learned that I also was in the early stages of Rheumatoid Arthritis. I'm thankful that God allowed me to find a less stressful style of living since my R.A. is aggravated by stress. So far the R.A. has been arrested by modern medical miracles.

You may be wondering if we considered Bear Valley an attractional church or a missional church. I'm not really sure which it was. When we met in an old shopping center next to a pawn shop, averaging 250, we were not very attractive; but 80% of our growth was through adult conversation. We didn't institutionalize our missional activities until finishing our building, but we did teach our people from the very start that they should find a place to volunteer in their community.

I remember Ted Freemon, one of our first adults to be baptized, calling me to ask where he could serve during his first Christmas as a believer. I suggested he take some homemade Christmas food to the police station, late at night on Christmas eve, and thank his local police for serving while others were free to spend time with family. Our goal was to send transformed people back into the community to serve transformationally.

I'm also concerned that many churches that consider themselves missional, fail to engage with the unchurched community in a way that adds them to a congregation of believers. Doing acts of love is not enough. Jesus said we must also baptize and teach.

If you lead a missional church, I would like to challenge you. How many attenders do you have that have not attended church in the last three years? If it is less than 30%, in my humble opinion, you probably should change something or start something.

There is so much which needs to be said about that last paragraph, for God calls some to be faithful servants without numerical success in their lifetime. Look at Abraham, Isaiah or Barnabas. Enough said for this book.

Finally, if you would like to join the conversation, find me on the internet:

www.samuelWcarmack.com

I've posted on this blog a selected bibliography I used with a Ph.D. seminar I taught about new paradigm churches.

Leave a comment on our Amazon page and Facebook page:

www.facebook/bearvalleyandme

ONE MORE THING:

The sub-title of the book has double meaning. We wanted to let the reader know that the story is told from the point of view of the wife, but it also refers to the husband. I am married to a church planter!

Acknowledgements

There are many people who made this story possible. It is virtually impossible to name each and every one. There are so many family members who supported us. There were some key individuals in the Southern Baptist Convention who made every effort to find funding during the first three years. Bob Roberts, the sponsoring pastor, is mentioned in the book, but I also found great encouragment and help from three other pastors: John Worcester, Harold Bullock and Doug Walker. Each of these helped in their own way and we owe them a loud note of thanks.

Many people helped with layout, proof-reading, editing, etc. A special thanks goes to Bailey Jo Carmack and Lorrie Cheney.

I also want to thank Jay Bruner. He was one of the church planters we helped. He needs to know how his gracious spirit was such a joy and encouragement.

www.ingramcontent.com/pod-product-compliance
Lightning Source LLC
Chambersburg PA
CBHW071459040426
42444CB00008B/1412